In Search of the Ninth Legion
(Legio VIIII Hispana)
The Archaeological Clues

Edited and Compiled by
Ian Dewar

'Quia Notitia'

This monograph attempts to gather the known archaeology pertaining to the Ninth Legion into a single archive, illustrated where possible by digital images, associated maps and other relevant artefacts. By considering evidence from known sites, camps, forts and battles of the Legio VIIII Hispano and adding some GIS mapping of their plans and location, it concludes with an analysis of credible theories for the Ninth Legion's mysterious disappearance with some thoughts and conclusions on their reliability.

For my Grandson

James Dewar-Tomlinson

Dedication

To all those still on patrol.

Acknowledgements

I am deeply indebted for the cooperation and kindness shown by several Museums and other academic organizations in releasing copyright images of artefacts relating to the Ninth Legion. In addition, I should like to thank numerous individuals who found time to assist me, especially Paula Avery who undertook much of the onerous reproduction of plans and coloured overlays (See Methodology). My appreciation goes also to the Friends of Malton Museum, London University, the Sanisera Archaeology Institute, the University of Strasbourg, University of Hull, York Archaeological Trust, Humber Archaeological Trust and the Barnet museum.

ISBN: 978-1-326-82693-2

www.maison-pigalle.com

Contents

List of Tables   5
List of Illustrations   5/6
List of Abbreviations   6

Part One

1. **Introduction:** Aims & Objectives   8

2. **Literary Review:**   9

3. **Methodology:**   14

4. **The Ninth Legion:**   18

Part Two

5. **Archaeological Evidence:** Literary
   Evidence/Epigraphic Evidence/Altars/Building
   Inscriptions/Other Inscriptions/Tombstones/
   Numismatic Evidence/Metalwork/Ceramic
   evidence/Weapons.

6. **Archaeological Sites in Great Britain: (**Occupied by
   the Ninth): Longthorpe/Newton on Trent/Leicester/
   Lincoln/London/Brough on Humber/Templebrough/

Slack (Huddersfield)/Castleford/York/Knewton Kyme/
Malton/Aldborough/Haelam Bridge/Catterick/Old
Carlisle/Scalesceugh/Carlisle/Stanwix.

7. **Archaeological Sites around the World** (Occupied
   by the Ninth): Zaragoza/Sisak/ Rome/Nijmegen/
   Lambaesis /Petra.

Part Three

8. **The Disappearance of the Ninth:** Landscape/
   Existing Theories/Britain/Nijmegen/Judea/Parthia.

9. **Supposition:** Plague in the East/Resurgence of
   Britain/A British War/The reign of Trajan/Reign of
   Hadrian and Hadrian's Wall   .

Part Four

1. Structure & Command
2. Officers of the Ninth.
3. Discussion: What happened to the Ninth?
4. Summary & Conclusion.
5. Bibliography.

Tables

Table 1: Postings of the Ninth legion   19
Table 2: The Campaign and Battles of the Ninth   20/21

Illustrations

Illustration 1: Inscription RIB 665   26
Illustration 2: Tombstone RIB 254   27
Illustration 3: Legionary denarii of Mark Anthony   29
Illustration 4: Denarius of Domitian 83AD issue   30
Illustration 5: Plan of the two forts at Longthorpe   36
Illustration 6: Plan of the fort at Newton on Trent   37
Illustration 7: GIS plan of the Lincoln fort   38
(Including a conjectural plan)
Illustration 8: Plan of the fort at Brough on Humber   39
Illustration 9: Plan of the fort at Templeborough   40
Illustration 10: GIS plan of the fort at Slack   41
Illustration 11: Plan of the fort at Castleford   42
Illustration 12: GIS phases of the fort at York   43
(Including a conjectural plan)
Illustration 13: Plan of the fort at Newton Kyme   44
Illustration 14: Plan of the fort at Malton   45
Illustration 15: Plan of Aldborough   46
Illustration 16: Plan of the fort at Healam Bridge   47
Illustration 17: Plan of the fort & Vicus at Catterick   48
Illustration 18: Plan of Old Carlisle   49

Illustration 19: Plan of Carlisle   50
Illustration 20: Plan of the fort at Nijmegen   52
Illustration 21: Plan of the fort at Lambaesis   53
Illustration 22: Plan of Petra showing the location of
the tomb of Lucius Aninius Sextus Florentinus   54

Abbreviations

CIL	Corpus Inscriptionum Latinurum
GIS	Geographical Information System
ILS	Inscriptiones Latinae Selectae
NAA	Neutron Activation Analysis
RIB	Roman Inscriptions of Britain
YAT	York Archaeological Trust

AD 2016

'Friends, Britons, Countrymen...' might be a more appropriate beginning if I were able to stand in a first century Forum and address the multitude of potential readers of this monograph? Alas, that is not to be. In its stead I will simply reveal and confess my interest in the Ninth Legion, or the 'Legio VIIII Hispana', has never waned since our first tenuous encounter in Rosemary Sutcliff's fine writings.

I'm not referring to Rosemary's excellent *'Eagle of the Ninth'* as one might imagine; but to her later yet no less enthralling Arthurian trilogy and that turbulent, adventure driven period in our island's history - following as it did the end of Rome's occupation. Arthur himself she reveals, was *'off the purple',* suggesting that legendary king was born of Roman nobility and I can only suppose that was the phrase that lodged somewhere in my subconscious, stimulating my burgeoning fascination in everything to do with Roman Britain - and the Ninth Legion in particular.

Let's face it, what warm blooded Scotsman couldn't be stirred by the possibility his forebears were instrumental in seeing the demise of an enemy's finest body of fighting men somewhere in the misty wilderness of his native land? But enough of this romanticism. Let us look anew at the loss of the Ninth Legion and consider further the archaeological evidence since uncovered...

Part One

1. Introduction:

In recent years considerable interest in the Ninth Legion has been generated by the publication of a number of books and films on the subject. Whilst this has undoubtedly raised the profile of the army in Roman Britain, it has also led to a distortion of known facts as many of the recent works have been works of fiction as opposed to new academic study or documentary. There has also been some small resurgence of interest from both amateur and professional archaeologists although - and perhaps surprisingly - given the public profile of the Ninth, there is still no single substantive study of the archaeological evidence relating to its service, campaigns and ultimate fate.

Aims & Objectives -

The aims and objectives herein must be to research and collate the known archaeological evidence relating to the Ninth Legion with some further analysis and interpretation to extend our understanding of the legion's many deployments and eventual demise.

It may also prove useful to conduct a brief literature review to identify relevant archaeological evidence pertaining to the Ninth Legion referred to in numerous archaeological papers, journals, books (factual and fiction), interim academic studies and excavation reports for known sites through internet sources and antiquarian catalogues of inscriptions.

Collating other evidence, including images of the relevant artefacts will help produce a digital archive of the legion and enable us consider the evidence from newly identified sites and/or sites potentially built or simply occupied by the Ninth.

Finally, we need to track the movement of the Ninth Legion throughout the world, applying GIS mapping to pre-existing plans and revealling its military bases in more detail. We can then evaluate many existing theories on the legion's disappearance in the light of evidence found. Finally, almost inevitably we must draw some appropriate conclusions.

2. Literary Review

The Ninth Legion's disappearance has been a popular subject for historical fiction, fantasy and yes, even science fiction novels - a tradition begun by Sutcliff (1954) when she published 'The Eagle of the Ninth'. The latter has been adapted many times in several formats, including a Home Service radio dramatization on Children's Hour (Sutcliff et al. 1956) and a TV serial (BBC 1977). In more recent years there has been a further radio dramatization, 'The Eagle of the Ninth', (Sutcliff & BBC Radio 4 1996) which in 2011 formed the basis of the movie *'The Eagle'* (MacDonald 2011).

Popular culture has resulted in numerous other fictional works based on the Ninth including the 1979 historical novel *'Legions of the Mists'* (Cockrell 1979) which recounts the destruction of the Ninth as a result of an attack by combined tribes in Scotland. In the novel *'The Shadowy Horses'* by Kearsley (1997), an archaeologist believes he has found the remains of a fort which housed the Ninth Legion in remote Eyemouth in Scotland, whilst in another historical novel, *'Last of the Ninth'* (Bennett 2010), the Ninth Legion is destroyed by the Parthian armies under General Chosroes in Cappadocia in AD 161. The latest work of fiction to cover the topic is the *'Eagle has Fallen'* (Young 2012), which depicts the Ninth Legion being destroyed by the Votadini, Brigantes and Carvetti in the Cheviot Hills in AD 117. This too has been adapted as a film. Two other recent films which portray the Ninth Legion are *'The Last Legion'* (Teale 2008) in which the Ninth Legion are still in Britain around AD 460 and *'Centurion'* (Marshall 2010) which is loosely based on the legendary massacre of the Ninth Legion in Caledonia in the early second century AD.

More reliable sources for a professional study include a number of primary writings from the late republic (Mid-first century BC to the beginning of Commodus' reign in AD 180). These are of significance for this research project in that they provide contemporary accounts on the whereabouts of several military units and key individuals on particular dates and therefore provide a foundation for the interpretation of archaeological finds. Several of these are discussed later under the heading 'Archaeological Evidence'.

Fortunately, Roman culture meant it was common to inscribe stone, ceramics and even domestic utensils with details of those who made them or fashioned them into tools, buildings and structures. These are recorded in a number of antiquarian catalogues which are referred to later in this book. Of particular value are tile stamps and tombstone inscriptions or engravings which frequently provide details of military service of a particular individual which again is of considerable value in tracking the likely movements of the Ninth Legion.

In terms of secondary contextual sources, Birley (2005) examines events in Britain during the reign of successive governors and details how the various legions were deployed. A comprehensive survey of the evolution and growth of the Roman army including the birth and demise of the Ninth is provided by Keppie (1998) whilst Webster (1985), examines the legion's military campaigns. Dando-Collins (2010) looks at the history of every Roman legion in detail - including the Ninth - and suggests what fate may have befallen each.

An easily accessible, general but nonetheless valuable introduction to those artefacts associated with the Ninth, their deployment or providing further information about the legion is provided by Sansom, writing for a non-academic web based audience (2010). By contrast, Betts' (1985) thesis focuses entirely on the brick and tile industry of the York area and provides detailed information on ceramics which augment the earlier work of Wright (1978), by examining tile stamps of the Ninth Legion. An understanding of this material is crucial in tracking the movements of the Ninth to and between various garrisons across Roman Britain. Similarly Sijpesteijn's (1996) discussion of the finds at Nijmegen in Holland provides much evidence of the Ninth's presence there at some point in their history.

Archaeological evidence for the movements of the Ninth is largely provided by excavation reporting. Where and when the various forts were built and occupied by the Ninth are also described as accurately as possible. The work of Bidwell & Hodgson (2009) helpfully covers all the British bases of the Ninth Legion, apart from Longthorpe, providing plans and other useful references while Bishop (2013a) gives us another valuable source of similar information on bases outside Britain material constantly updated via the author's associated website (Bishop 2013b).

Interestingly, until the early 1950's there appears to have been a general acceptance by archaeologists that the Ninth

12

met its end somewhere in Northern Britain in the early part of second century (Wright 1948). However, Sutcliff's fictional account which largely came to the same conclusion, whilst clearly containing a number of errors seems to have had the effect of spurring some archaeologists to propose alternative theories based on 'new' archaeological evidence. During the 1960s, the work of Bogaers & Haalebos (1979) constituted the first credible alternative when it led to a suggestion the Ninth Legion had been based at Nijmegen in Holland from c.AD 121-130 before being destroyed at a later date in Judea. This was supported by Mor (1986) and despite the fact he later concluded the evidence in fact pointed to the Twenty Second Legion and not the Ninth being annihilated in Judea, his theory remains the cause of much debate. In the same decade Birley (1981) among others proposed the Ninth Legion had been destroyed in the Parthian Wars of AD 161-162. Finally, Ritterling (1925) took a 'prosopographical' approach in studying the fate of the Ninth and concluded that there may have been heavy casualties in the German War of Marcus Aurelius; but well after the Legion had left Nijmegen?

Within the last decade there have been other signs of a resurgence of interest in the fate of the Ninth with an important addition to the debate being made by Driessen (2009) whose work reinterprets the archaeology of Nijmegen. Similarly, Faulkner (2001) has brought forward a suggestion first made by AR Birley that there is evidence for the Legion being involved in the construction of part of Hadrian's Wall which may impact on views as to the Legion's most likely movements. Dando-Collins (2010) has also cast some doubt on the Parthian War theory. Most recently, Russell (2010) summarised the evidence (or lack of it) and concluded the most likely outcome is the Ninth Legion disappeared in Britain sometime within the second or third decade of the second century AD. The ongoing debate and some recent developments in archaeological evidence will be addressed in greater detail in the final section of the book.

3. Methodology

In addition to researching relevant publications, reports and online articles, the literature 'review' involved identifying inscriptions relating to the Ninth in all three volumes of 'Roman Inscriptions of Britain (RIB)' (Collingwood & Wright 1983), (Collingwood R.G. & Wright R.P. 1995), (Hassall et al. 2009) and all seventeen volumes of 'Corpus Inscriptionum Latinarum (CIL)' (Alföldy & Preussische Akademie der Wissenschaften 1995) plus three volumes of 'Inscriptiones Latinae Selectae (ILS)' (Dessau 2009). 'The Fasti of Roman Britain' (Birley 1981) was also helpful in identifying people who served in the Ninth legion at all ranks from standard bearers Optio to Legate; and provides useful details of their earlier and later career fortunes.

The relevant ILS and CILs (which are published in Latin) were translated using Google translate packages along with several publications which were in other languages such as the archaeological reports for Nijmegen in Holland which was in several regional dialects and throughout, regular checks were made of all available sources to search for new information, or new interpretations on evidence of the Ninth Legion. The literature review was also used to research existing theories about the legion's disappearance. These theories are discussed later where they are evaluated against the evidence that supports or disproves them.

A list of all existing categories of evidence belonging to the Ninth Legion (ceramic finds, stamped tiles, tombstones, funerary inscriptions, metalwork, temple dedications, altars, building inscriptions, coins, equipment and weaponry) was compiled as a Microsoft Excel spreadsheet identifying where and when they were found and specifying in which museums they are currently located. Individuals and museum were then contacted by email with requests for digital images of the artefact(s). Visits were also made to the Yorkshire Museum and the Dig Hungate Museum and Roman Baths site in York. Other visits were to *The Collection of Art and Archaeology in Lincolnshire* at Lincoln and the Malton Museum to obtain relevant photographs. This proved more difficult at Malton where the museum building has temporary space limitations and artefacts had to be viewed at a storage facility by arrangement with local volunteers.

Plans of the relevant forts, fortlets and of vexilation fortresses were identified through archaeological reports and publications along with other relevant material. These were scanned and images digitized as TIFF files so that they could be imported into Arch GIS software. In Arch Maps 10, several folders were created to store fort plans, OS Base maps and Shape files. These are linked by pathways to the main document which is titled VIIII Legion Forts.

Beginning with Roman York (Eburacum) the 4 OS base maps were obtained and then imported into Arch Maps 10 by clicking on file; add data add OS base map after first changing the grid system to British National grid (or whichever country the site is in). Next a plan of the known archaeology of the roman fortress at York was added over the base map, after which some geo-referencing was done by adding control points (at least 6-8 were used for greater accuracy) then 'update geo referencing' was applied to ensure the image would be correctly positioned.

Fields were then added using 'snapping' so that the plan could be phased and labelled. The outer walls of the fort were snapped using polygons as were the ditches. The roads and sewers were then snapped using polylines as was each building inside the fort along with the hypercaust and flooring. Edits were saved every couple of steps so that nothing was lost or needed to be repeated.

A more up to date excavation plan was applied over the bathhouse which had more details plotted on them using the snapping and editing tool. A plan of the suggested building outlines within the fort produced by the York Archaeological Trust (YAT) was imported and an updated plan from the recent excavation under the Minster was also added.

For phasing, each diagram has the fortress or vexilation fortlet plan shown with each building in a different colour for different phases or periods of occupation. This was set up by opening up the attribute table and clicking 'add phase' and selecting the same colour, then right clicking on 'York' which has three phases encoded in different colours for the entirety of the fort. When the phasing was complete the edits were saved.

3.1b 'Colouring' lines: Original lines were coloured by in the attribute table selecting symbology, before selecting a different density for each phase then selecting the thickness of the line clicking 'apply' and 'ok'.

3.1c Interpretation and Labelling: The attribute table and select phases were then used to add dates and other information for the key. At this point individual features for example 'corner tower' were labelled. A key and attribute table and direction arrow were then added as was a scale at the bottom which automatically adjusts as the user zooms in and out. This process was then repeated for Lincoln, Malton, Longthorpe, Nijmegen, Haelam Bridge, Slack (Huddersfield), Catterick, Castleford, Knewton Kyme, Templebrough, Brough on Humber, Aldborough and Scalesceugh, thus providing a series of individual phased plans.

4. The Ninth Legion

The origin of the Ninth Legion lies in the first century BC. However there is some dispute as to whether its founder was Gnaeus Pompeius Magnus (Pompey the Great) or Gaius Julius Caesar. (Dando-Collins 2010, p.150) suggests the 'Legion was raised, along with the 6th, 7th and 8th, by Pompey in Hispania in 65 BC'. However, sources describe Pompey as being in Iberia in 65 BC (Greenhalgh 1980, pp.101–4) and in Roman times this referred to the Bosphorus not Spain. In fact the first literary mention of the Legion comes in Caesar's *'Gallic Wars'* where he describes finding the Ninth stationed in Gaul in 59/8 BC (Keppie 1998, p.208) shortly after his appointment as Governor of Transalpine Gaul (Southern France). Caesar had been Praetor (from 63 to 62 BC) and then Governor (from 61 to 59 BC) of Hispania and it seems more likely that he raised the Legion then. Furthermore (Keppie 1998) and others argue that Julius Caesar was the founder of the legion as all battle records for the Ninth during the early years of the Legion's existence suggest that Caesar not Pompey was in control. During the Legion's long history they were also posted to locations in modern day Europe Africa and Britain taking part in several engagements. As far as records exist, these are detailed here.

Location	Dates	Source(s)
Spain	65/61 to 59 BC	(Olly & Aspin 2011)
Gaul	58-51 BC	ditto
Britain	55-54 BC	ditto
Macedonia	49-48 BC	ditto
Africa	48-45 BC	ditto
Zaragoza, Spain	45-43 BC	ditto
Siscia, Pannonia	43-35 BC	ditto
Illyricum	35-33 BC	ditto
Northern Spain	29-19 BC	ditto
Siscia, Pannonia	19 BC-AD 17	ditto
Africa	AD 17-23	ditto
Siscia, Pannonia	AD 23-43	ditto
Longthorpe	AD 43- 65	ditto
Lincoln	AD 65-71	ditto
York	AD 71-108	ditto
Nijmegen	AD 82-84	ditto
Carlisle	AD 108-122	ditto
Caesar's Gallic Wars	58-51 BC	Gallic tribes

		defeated
Caesar's 2nd Invasion of Britain	5-4 BC	
Battle of Gergovia (Vercingetorix)	5-2 BC	Roman Defeat
Revolt at Seige of Alesia	5-2 BC	Roman Victory
Caesar's Civil Wars: Battle of Ilerda. Battles of Dyrrhachium 2nd Battle of Dyrrhachium Battle of Pharsalus. Battles of Ruspina and Thapsus and Battle of Munda	49-48 BC 46-45 BC	After 2nd battle of Dyrrhachium, Titus Labienus executed all the prisoners from the 9th legion. At the battle of Munda, Labienus died at the hands of the Ninth and after the battle they cremated him on the battlefield.
Liberator's Civil War 2nd Battle of Philippi	42 BC	
Sicillian Revolt: Battle of Naulochus	36 BC	
Final War of the Roman Republic: Battle of Actium	31 BC	

Cantabrian Wars	29-19 BC	
Pannonian War	AD 6-9	
Tacfarinus	AD 17-23	
Roman Invasion of Britain: Battle of the River Medway, Battle of Colchester and capturing city Battle of Caer Caradoc, Shropshire	AD 43-50	
Brigantian Civil War	AD 57	
Boudican Revolt: Ambushed en route to Colchester. They lost 2000 men and retreated to their old base at Longthorpe.	AD 60-61	
Battle of Bedriacum Battle of Cremona	AD 68-69	
2nd Brigantian Civil War	AD 69-71	
Agricola's British Campaigns: Battle of Mons Grapius	AD 77-84	

The Ninth Legion was retired and pensioned off soon after the end of the Civil war. However, when Caesar was assassinated the legion was reformed and heavily involved in the Liberator's Civil War (43-2 BC).

From AD107-8 records show the Ninth was very much involved rebuilding the walls of their fortress at York - only this time in stone. RIB 665 (Collingwood & Wright 1983, p.223) However after AD 108 no definitive record of the Legion has been found and its fate from that time remains uncertain. It is known that towards the end of Trajan's reign and the beginning of Hadrian's (AD 110's-120's) there were at least four British revolts and rebellions; and it is likely the legion was involved to some degree in each of these. What is clear is that by AD 122 the Sixth Victrix and not the Ninth Legion were stationed at York.

Nomenclature:

The Ninth Legion is often referred to as the IX or VIIII by its roman numeric. Numeric VIIII is rarely used in later texts but was a valid recording of the period. Throughout its lifetime the Ninth Legion was known by several different names and titles. The earliest of these is the IX Victrix (the Victorious Ninth) which was given to them by Caesar during the Gallic Wars after Vercingetorix surrendered at the end of the siege of Alesia in 52 BC. At this time the legion's silver eagle was replaced with a gilded one, reputedly paid for out of Caesar's own purse (Caesar, Book VII, sect. 89.).

In 45 BC, by the end of the Civil War between Pompey and Caesar the legion was known as the IX Macedonica and it has been suggested that this title was bestowed to them after the victory at Pharsalus in 47 BC (ILS928) The emperor Augustus later awarded them the title the IX Hispana (Legio Hispana VIIII) after their service during the Cantabrian Wars and this is the title by which they are most commonly known.

An inscription found in Athens (ILS928) on a Tombstone belonging to Lucius Aquillius Pompaeus Florus, identifies him as a military tribune of the IX Victrix, Macedonica and Hispana. It is unusual that all three previous names are mentioned though a further name, the 'Hispaniensis' is found on a tombstone (ILS3221) belonging to Marcus Aemilius Marcus Pobeus, described as a cavalry commander, veteran of Legio IX Hispaniensis (stationed in Spain). It was found in North Africa at Calibus and probably dates from the period when the Ninth Legion was stationed in Africa during the Tacfarinas Revolt AD 17-24. For the purpose of this report the Hispana VIIII will be referred to as the Ninth Legion and vice-versa.

-:.:-

Part Two

5. Archaeological Evidence

As the title of this work suggests, extensive efforts have been made to identify artefacts related to the Ninth, to establish their current location and to obtain digital images for inclusion with permissions from relevant museums. More information on the artefacts described can be easily sourced on the web (Roman Britain) with information relating to where and when they were found, where they are currently housed and other relevant referencing data.

Literary Evidence exist from a number of primary sources containing contemporary accounts, all relevant to this study. Julius Caesar's commentaries on the Gallic and civil wars provide detailed information on the Ninth Legion's origins, early campaigns and battles. Cornelius Tacitus's *'Annals'*, *'Histories'* and *'The Life of Agricola'* provide an insightful history of the Roman Empire from the reign of Tiberius to that of Nero (AD 14-68) while the Histories adequately cover the Year of Four Emperors following the downfall of Nero, the rise of Vespasian and the rule of the Flavian Dynasty (69–96) up to the death of Domitian. These two works detail the Ninth Legion's part in the invasion of Britain, the Boudican revolt, the Brigantian revolts and the Chatian wars. Agricola retells the life of Tacitus's father-in-law Gnaeus Julius Agricola, an eminent Roman general and much relevant for the coverage of the Boudican revolt. Agricola was governor of Britain from

AD 77-84 during which period he completed the conquest of Wales, conquered Northern England and Scotland as far as the Grampians. He also defeated a large Caledonian army at the battle of Mons Graupius - all of which involved the Ninth Legion.

Dio Cassius' 88 - volume Roman History covers the same events as Tacitus and Caesar although possibly (at least for the period which concerns this report) without the personal bias and with the benefit of a degree of historical perspective as it was written during the Third century AD. Gaius Suetonius's Life of the Twelve Caesars, which spans the period from Julius Caesar to the end of Domitian's reign, provides information on events in various parts of the empire including Britain. Titus Livy's 'History of Rome' is particularly helpful in describing the Ninth Legion's campaigns and battles after Caesar's assassination and during the early years of Augustus' reign. Finally, the correspondence of Marcus Cornelius Fronto with Marcus Aurelius Antoninus, Lucius Verus, Antoninus Pius, and various friends provides a valuable reference to military losses in parts of the empire.

Several altars have been located in Roman Europe which have been dedicated by members of the Ninth Legion to gods and deities. Two altars were located in York. One, RIB 644 (Collingwood & Wright 1983, p.216) is dedicated to Fortuna by Sosia Iuncina the wife of Quintus Anthony Isaurici, Legate of the Ninth Legion and the second (RIB 659)

(Collingwood & Wright 1983, p.221) to the god Silvanus by Lucius Celerinius Vitalis, a staff clerk of the Ninth Legion. Another altar found at Aachen-Burtschield near Nijmegen in Holland was dedicated to Apollo by Lucius Latinius Macer. This inscription tells us Lucius was initially of the first file of the First Cohort of Leg VIIII Hispana, then a 'first spear' (senior centurion) of the Ninth Legion and after that, camp prefect of the Ninth Legion. Lucius erected the altar on behalf of himself and his men (881147) (Alföldy & Preussische Akademie der Wissenschaften 1995). This stone tablet (See illustration below) was found by workmen in 1854 at York.

Illustration 1: Inscription RIB 665

The Emperor Caesar
Nerva Trajan Augustus, son of the deified Nerva, Conqueror of Germany, Conqueror of Dacia, pontifex maximus, in his twelfth year of tribunician power, six times acclaimed emperor, five times consul, father of his country, built this gate by the agency of the Ninth Legion Hispana.

The tablet was uncovered in King's Square near the South East gateway of the roman fort and has since been restored and dated to AD 107-8 based on the information it contains.

A further inscription (ILS 1025) from Tivoli, Italy mentions a Lucius Roscius Aelianus Maecius Celer, son of Marcus, of the tribe Quirina; Military Tribune in Legion IX Hispana, and also serving in a detachment of the Legion in the German Campaign in AD 83 (Burn 1969, pp.32–33). Another, (ILS 9485) at Antioch in Pisidia mentions a Gaius Caristanius Fronto, as son of Gaius of the tribe Sergia, a Legate commanding Legion IX Hispana in Britain during the reign of Domitian (Burn 1969, pp.29–30).

Five tombstones belonging to the Ninth Legion have been found at Lincoln one of which belonged to Quintus Cornelius a trooper of the Ninth Legion who served in the century of Cassius Matialis; with 19 years of service he died aged 40 (RIB 254, now lost, see Illustration 2 below) (Collingwood & Wright 1983, p.84).

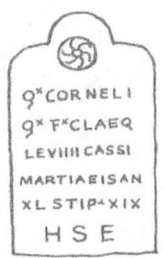

Gaius Saufeius a soldier of the Ninth had given twenty two years of service when he died aged 40 (RIB 255) (Collingwood & Wright 1983, p.84) whilst Lucius Sempronius Flavius a soldier of the Ninth Legion who served in the time of Babudius Severus, had seven years of service by the time he died aged 30 (RIB 256) (Collingwood & Wright 1983, p.85). Four fragments of the tombstone of Gaius Valerius, a soldier of the Ninth Legion and standard bearer of the Century of Hospes, reveals he had fourteen years of service and died aged 35 (RIB 257) (Collingwood & Wright 1983, p.85). Similarly, three fragments of a gabled tombstone of Marcus ... s, son of Marcus a soldier of the Ninth Legion (RIB 260) were found in Lincoln (Collingwood & Wright 1983, p.86). Further, at York two tombstones have been found, one belonging to Lucius Duccius Rufinus, a standard-bearer of the Ninth Legion aged 28 from Vienne (RIB 673) (Collingwood & Wright 1983, p.226) This has a carving depicting Lucius holding a maniple standard with medallions and a record book above the inscription. The second York tombstone was erected by the heirs of Gaius son of Gaius ..? (either a soldier or officer) of the Ninth Legion Hispana and tells us that he survived his twenty five years service (normal service period in a legion) and died in retirement in York. Gaius originally came from Milan (RIB 680) (Collingwood & Wright 1983, p.229).

Three coins have been found throughout the roman world which are clearly attributable to the Ninth Legion. Two coins have been excavated at Zaragoza in Spain where it is known the Ninth Legion's veterans were settled by Caesar after he disbanded them (Livy 2012) These two coins shown in Illustration #3 are Legionary denarii of Mark Anthony from the late republic.

Legionary denarii of Mark Anthony: Obverse: ANT AVG III VIR R P C, depicting a galley. Reverse: LEG VIIII, depicting an Aquila and two legionary standards.
(Forum Ancient Coins 2013)

The third coin was found at Nijmegen in Holland, during the re excavation of the roman fort (Driessen 2009) which depicts Domitian and bears the stamp of the Ninth Legion. The coin, which is depicted in Illustration #4 below, dates to AD 83.

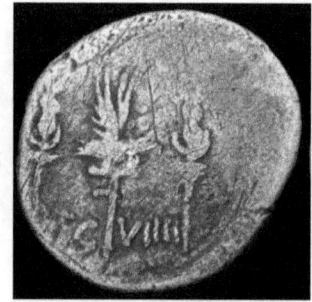

Denarius of Domitian AD 83 issue (Driessen 2009)

A spear head was found in York in a Cerialan deposit (Quintus Petilius Cerialis Caesius Rufus, Governor of Britain AD 71-74) during excavations under York Minster. This was in the undercroft during 2013 to make way for the 'Revealing York Minster' exhibition. At Lincoln, a centurion's phalera (military decoration) and a horse hair crest mount have been found along with a pugio in its scabbard. These were found in a deposit belonging to the period when Lincoln was occupied by the Ninth Legion (Jones 2002). A local detectorist found a ballista bolt head or dog tag with VIIII on one side at Teviothead in the Scottish borders which, at the time of its production would have been in the territory of the Brigantes (Moffatt 2013)and finally, at Ewijk near Nijmegen in

Holland, a phalera (horse harness decoration) pendant stamped Leg IX Hisp was discovered during the excavation of a large villa site (Sijpesteijn, 1996).

That said, the most numerous types of evidence for the Ninth Legion are ceramic objects including tiles, imbrexs, tegulae, mortaria and tile tombs. However, ceramic evidence cannot be accurately dated and therefore NAA and thin section analysis have been used by archaeologists to derive information such as where they were made, their chemical composition and where the constituent materials originated. At York the legionary tile kilns were situated on Brick Clays on Aldwark road and at Peasholme Green. A total of eighty two ceramic artefacts have been recovered from the fort and vicus at York (Research indicates thirty eight from York itself?) and have been identified as belonging to the Ninth Legion due to the stamps they bear. These consist of one flue tile fragment, one voussoir fragment, twelve bricks, twenty three imbrexs and forty five tegulae. Most of these are the property of the Yorkshire Museum and York Minster, although four of them are in Sheffield Museum and another in Hull & East Riding Museum. Another is in the British Museum and a fine example is in the great North Museum in Newcastle. These provide testament to the Ninth Legion's founding of York and their long period of occupation of the site. The stamps on the York tiles (following) are described in more detail by R.P. Wright in Volume 2 Fascule 4 (Collingwood R.G. & Wright R.P. 1995, pp.167-74):

RIB 2462.5: tile stamped Leg·IX·Hisp
RIB 2462.6: tegula & imbrex (roof tiles) stamped Leg·IX·Hisp
RIB 2462.7: tegulae and a brick stamped Leg·IX·Hisp
RIB 2462.8: tegulae and flue tile fragment stamped Hisp
RIB 2462.9: tegula from tomb I stamped Leg·IX·Hisp
RIB 2462.9a: brick stamped leg IX Hisp
RIB 2462.9b: tegula stamped Leg·IX·Hisp
RIB 2462.9c: brick stamped leg IX Hisp
RIB 2462.10: fragment of tegula stamped Hisp
RIB 2462.11: tegula and voussoir fragment stamped
Leg·IX·Hisp
RIB 2462.12: tile and tegula stamped Leg·IX·Hisp
RIB 2462.17: brick stamped leg IX Vic

Outside of York, at the Iron Age Hillfort of Stanwick in North Yorkshire, a tile stamped LEG IX HISP was uncovered At Aldborough, an imbrex, brick and tegula were found during excavations there and are all stamped LEG IX HISP and currently housed in Liverpool, Aldborough and Leeds museums. At Malton, three tiles were found in a Trajanic deposit, two of which are from die stamp 13 (as classified by Wright) and the others are die stamp 12 which are stamped Le, X HIS and IX H which can be assumed as LEG IX HISP.

A fragment of tile was also found at Dalton Parlours Villa where it had been reused. The Tile may have come from the fort at Knewton Kyme or Tadcaster. To the North West, In Carlisle, two tiles were discovered and stamped with LEG V and LEG VIIII H whereas, nearby at Stanwix in Cumbria, a tile stamped LEG VIIII H was also discovered. The three previously mentioned tiles were made at Scalesceugh using the same die as a tile working on the road to Carlisle. Additionally, a tile stamped LEG VI and LEG VIIII H has been found at this site.

At Castleford, West Yorkshire, seven bricks have been found, six were found in 1978 during the excavation of the Roman baths in the fort annex which are classified as RIB246.9 and one was found recently in the vicus. These tiles are stamped with HISP, X HISP, IX HISP. Two are stamped with LE and another two with LEG IX: all of which can be reconstructed as LEG IX HISP. From Slack (?) in Huddersfield, two tegulae and a brick stamped Leg IX HISP were located during the brief excavation of the fort before the site was built on. Also in Yorkshire, a tile with G VIIII HI stamped on it which can be restored as LEG VIIII HISP was found at Doncaster in the North Eastern corner of the Flavian fort in a Hadriani demolition layer; and a brick stamped with LEG IX HISP was found at Templeborough near Rotherham.

A single tile was found at Old Winteringham, south of the River Humber and was stamped with the same die as the one from Templeborough. At Lincoln, bricks and tiles stamped LEG IX HISP were found such the one excavated in 1910 and on display in the Collection in Lincoln. A single tile at Hilly Wood near the fortress of Longthorpe in

Northamptonshire was stamped with die 11. At Leicester a tile stamped LVIII was found and has been reconstructed as LVIIII HISP and lastly in England, a rim of a brownish red mortaria found in London, pre 1949, in Thames Street. This has graffiti scratched on it with a stylus which reads, Property of ..., Imaginifer of Legio IX (Wright 1978) and (Betts 1985).

A number of tiles, fragments and what appear to be tombstone covers have been unearthed during the current (2015-16) construction of London's CrossRail project but details of these are unavailable at the time of writing. Indications are these will contribute significantly to our knowledge of legionary life in the capital.

Finally, two brick fragments found at Nijmegen in Holland in 1963 are stamped LEG VIIII & II HI which has been restored as LEG VIIII HISP (Haalebos 2000, pp.12–13).

Apart from the pugio and spearhead mentioned above and a possible ballista bolt head, several stone ballista balls have been found at York beneath the Minster which consist of one small stone balls (26kg), one medium stone ball (52kg) and a large stone ball (78kg). The first two would have been used against enemy warriors, whereas the larger one would have been used against siege towers and battering rams (Ottaway 2004) and (Wilkins 2003, p.7).

6. Archaeological Sites in Great Britain:

A large number of military bases are known to have been occupied by the Ninth Legion, some of which have been extensively excavated whilst others are little more than a reference or interpretation from an aerial photograph. The available dating evidence below using GIS mapping to augment existing plans, clearly reveals building phases and important finds. The forts are analysed in chronological order to help track the legion's movements. (Bidwell & Hodgson 2009) and provide a more succinct and detailed analysis of each site (Bishop 2013a).

The fort at Longthorpe (overleaf) is located west of Peterborough and was discovered from aerial photography in 1960/61. The site was first excavated from 1967-73 and the original fortress found to be fronted on all sides by a double ditch system forming an area of almost exactly twenty five acres, enough room to comfortably house half the legion.

Longthorpe may have been built as early as AD 44 prior to the campaign against the Coritani of Lincolns and briefly reoccupied during the Boudican revolt of AD 60-61. There is also evidence of occupation for some time after the Romans left Britain.

Illustration #5: Plan of the two forts at Longthorpe (Frere et al. 1974, p.9)

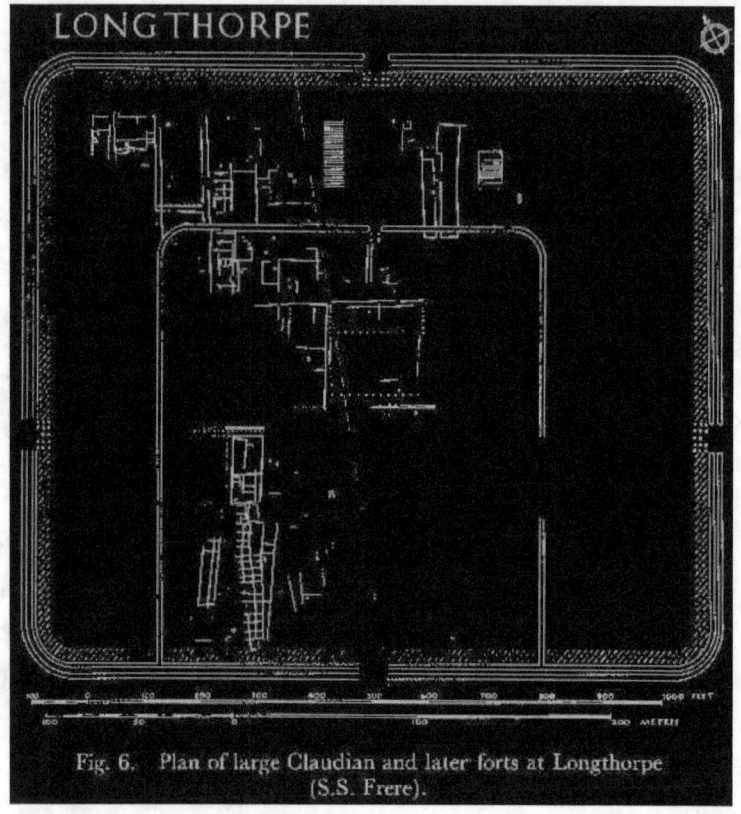

Fig. 6. Plan of large Claudian and later forts at Longthorpe
(S.S. Frere).

It has been suggested (Frere et al. 1974) at the same time Longthorpe was occupied, the other half of the legion was based at Newton on Trent. However the fort which is shown to the east of the meander in the River Trent in Illustration #6 has barely been excavated and to date nothing mentioning the Ninth legion or identified as belonging to them has been found at the site.

Illustration #6: Plan of the location of the fort at Newton on Trent
(Royal Commission on Historical Monuments 1995)

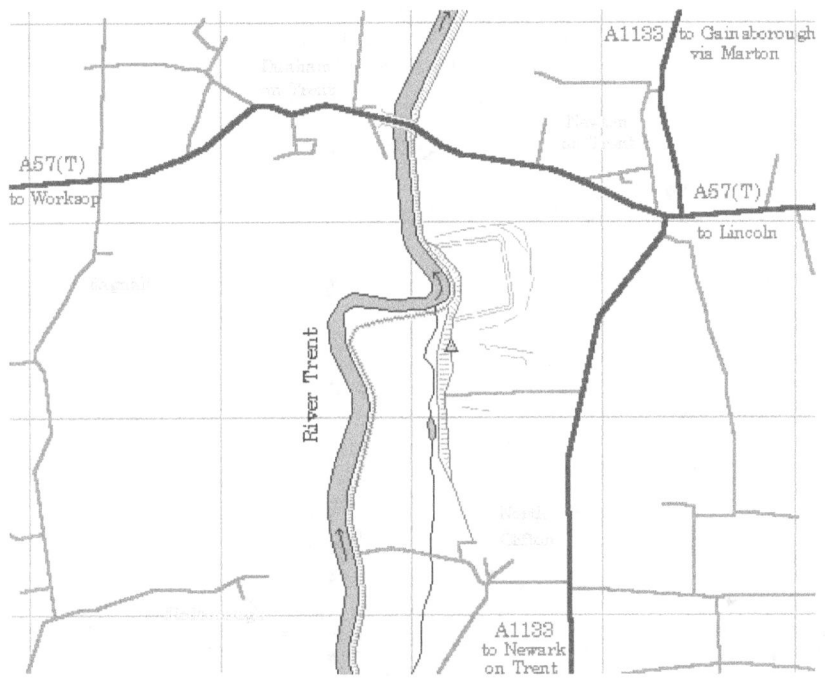

A tile that may have been the property of the Ninth Legion (See previous ceramics section) found at Leicester may well indicate a further possible fort site.

The fortress at Lincoln was aligned east-west and consisted of a single ditch and rampart enclosing an area of approximately forty one acres. This legionary fortress had originally been established as the base of Legio IX Hispana c.AD 60 although by AD 71 the Ninth had in fact moved to York (Ottaway 2004).

The highlighted areas below show those areas which have been excavated to date.

Illustration 7: GIS plan of the fort at Lincoln including a conjectural plan (Author) and (Bishop 2013a, p.82)

Plan of the Roman Fort at Lincoln

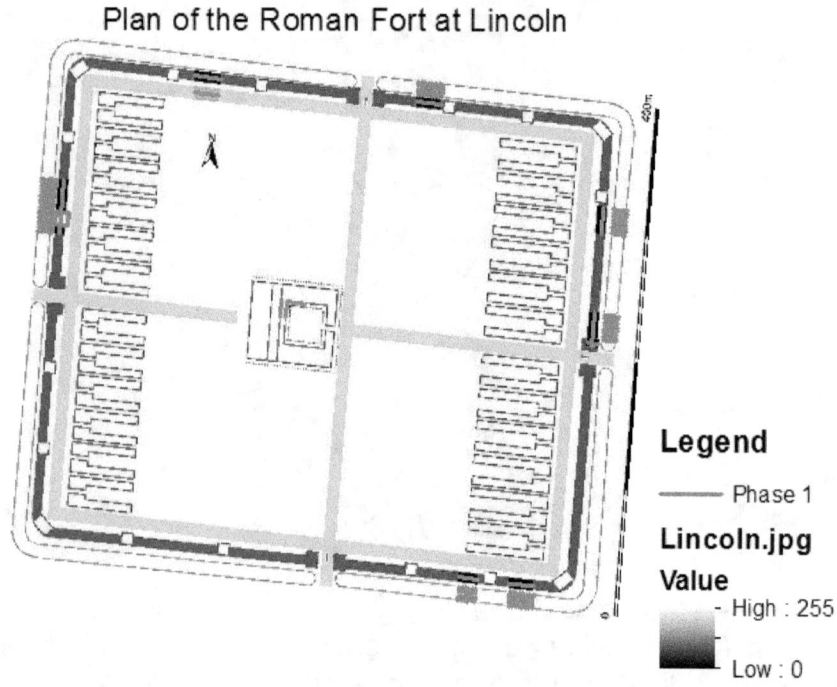

Legend

——— Phase 1

Lincoln.jpg

Value

High : 255

Low : 0

It has been suggested that the rim of a brownish red mortaria found in Thames Street, London may have been taken by a member of the Boudican revolt when they ambushed the Ninth legion on its way to Colchester and was subsequently dropped and broken during the sacking of London (Askew 1949).

Only the small section (highlighted below) of the fort from the Flavian period has been excavated at Brough, where a single tile bearing the name of the Ninth Legion has been found (Bidwell & Hodgson 2009, pp.177–180).

Illustration 8: Plan of the fort at Brough on Humber
(Bidwell & Hodgson 2009, p.178)

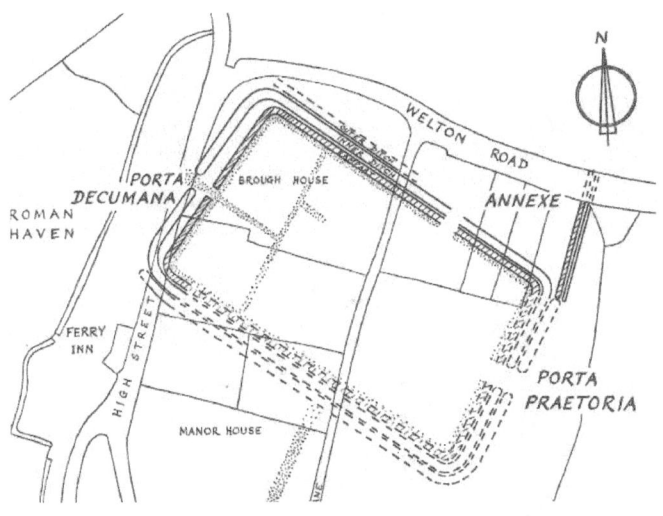

As shown in Illustration #9 (below) the Roman fort found at Templebrough is almost square, covering an area of five and a half acres. The occupation date of the fort is not certain but cannot be later than early Flavian. It may be earlier and it has been suggested this was built by the Ninth Legion also (Bidwell & Hodgson 2009, pp.91–93).

Ilustration 9: Plan of the fort at Templeborough
(Bidwell & Hodgson 2009, p.92)

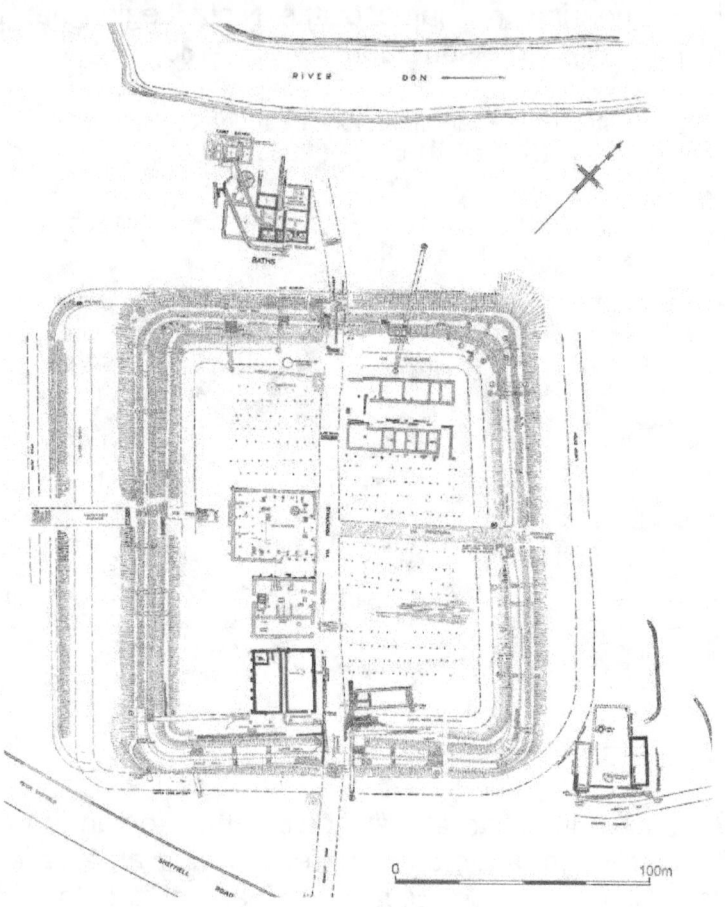

Another fort at Slack occupies an area of just 1½ acres This fort was constructed during the Flavian period, probably c.AD 80 but appears to have been abandoned before work was complete (as highlighted in Illustration #10) possibly because the auxiliary garrison (fourth cohort of Gauls) that replaced the vexilation of the Ninth Legion had been moved to the northern frontier (Bidwell & Hodgson 2009, pp.75–77)

Illustration #10: GIS plan of the fort at Slack
(Author with Bidwell & Hodgson 2009, p.76)

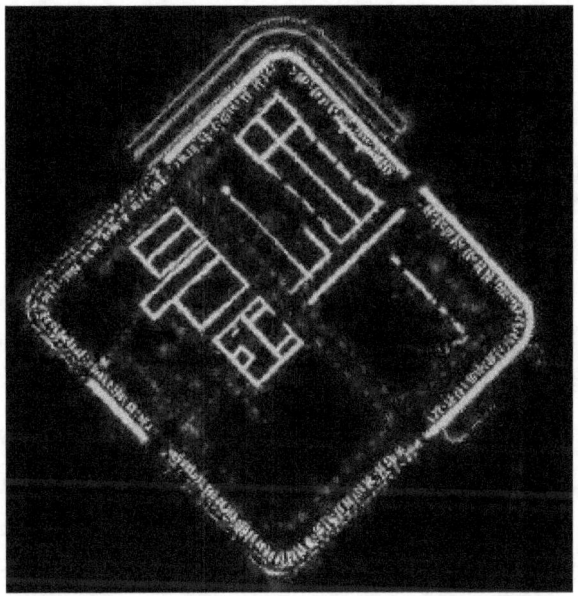

The Roman fortifications at Castleford have only been excavated in parts. To date the commander's house, a few barrack blocks, workshops and granaries and a bath house in the annex where tiles from the Ninth Legion were found are highlighted below. Illustration #11 (Bidwell & Hodgson 2009, pp.133–136).

Illustration #11: Plan of the fort at Castleford
(Bidwell & Hodgson 2009, p.134)

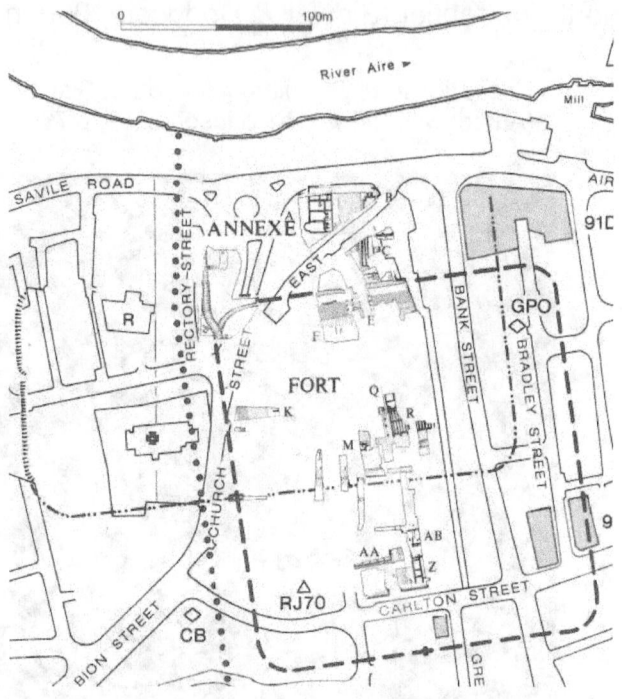

The defences of the original palisade fortress at York constructed during Cerealis' early campaigns against the Brigantes were replaced by stone walls by the Ninth Legion during the reign of the emperor Trajan in either late AD 107 or 108. Prior to this date the interior buildings were all of timber and tile construction. York has been thoroughly excavated and Illustration #12 shows the various phases of construction and conjectured outlines of buildings.

Illustration #12: GIS plan of the fort at York and a conjectural plan
(Ottaway 1996, fig.186)

(Phase #1-3 are highlighted below, although phase #3 and parts of the conjectural angular towers (bottom left) are not relevant to the Ninth).

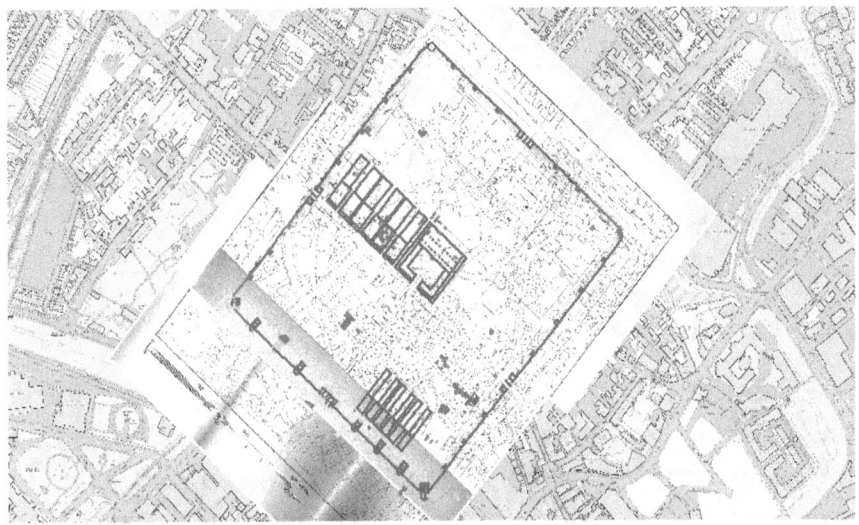

The Roman fort at Newton Kyme lies on the south bank of the River Wharfe, and was identified by aerial photography in 1949 as shown on Illustration #13. Lying just east of the spot where the Roman Road from Lincoln to Aldborough forded the stream, its size (Bidwell & Hodgson 2009, pp.136–138) suggested it was occupied by both legionaries and auxiliaries at the same time during the Agricolan period.

Illustration #13: Plan of the fort at Newton Kyme
(Bidwell & Hodgson 2009, p.137)

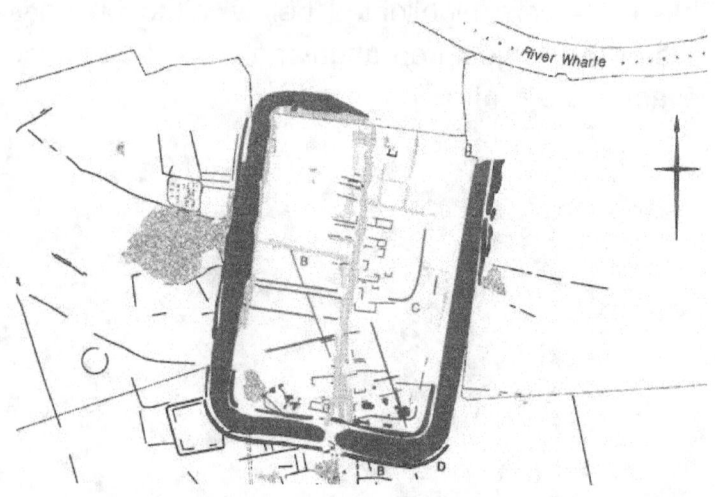

The fort at Malton (see Illustration #14) is thought to be an Agricolan vexilation fortress built by the Ninth Legion due to the finding of tiles belonging to the Legion and parts of armour, a sword ballista bolts and slingshot at the site. The footprint of The Derventio fort is big by Roman standards. It may have been an important staging post for troops marching to and from Hadrian's Wall. In Roman times the Derwent may have been navigable as far as Malton. The fort was also strategically placed to control the crossing of the river.

Illustration #14 of the fort at Malton
(Wenham 1974, p.49).

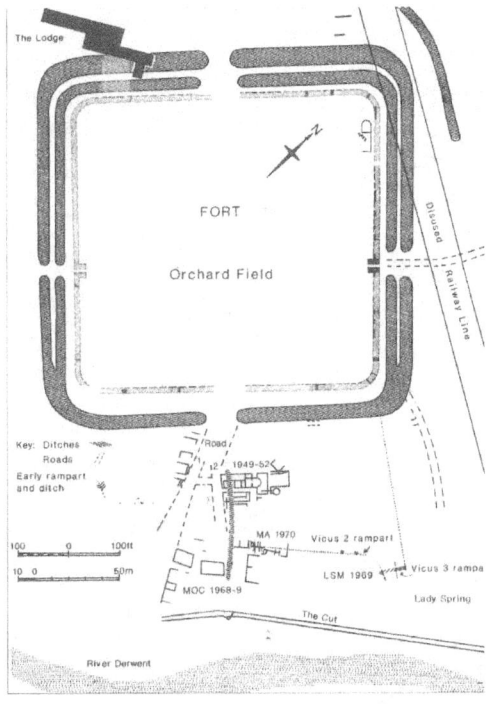

Although no firm evidence of a fort has been found at Aldborough, (Illustration #15) it seems likely there would have been one at the civitas capital of the Brigantes. A tile belonging to the Ninth was uncovered in Aldborough together with other military artefacts of the period.

Illustration #15 possible fort lines at Aldborough
(Bidwell & Hodgson 2009, p.140).

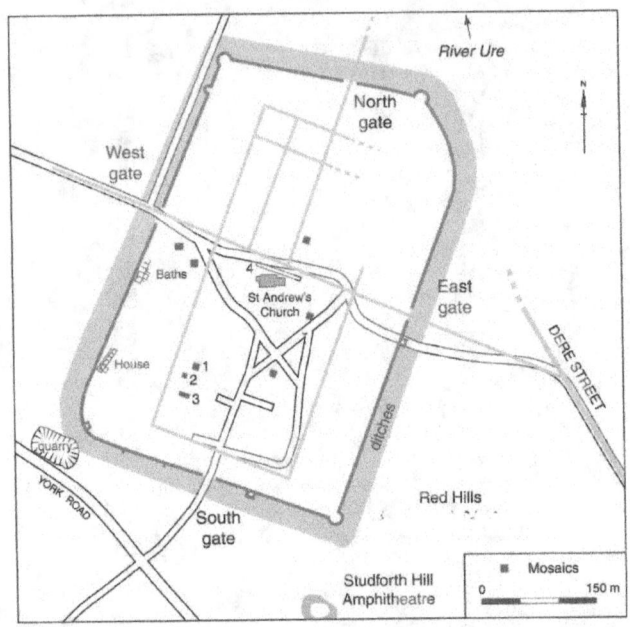

Healam Bridge located on the road between Aldborough
and Catterick was excavated in 1993/4 (Highways Agency
1994) and is believed to have been occupied by at least a
detachment of legionaries of the Ninth Legion from their base
at York at some time during the first century AD. Illustration
#16 shows the extent of the fort and adjacent industrial
complex which are bisected by the A1 Trunk road.

Illustration 16: Plan of the fort at Healam Bridge
(Highways Agency 1994)

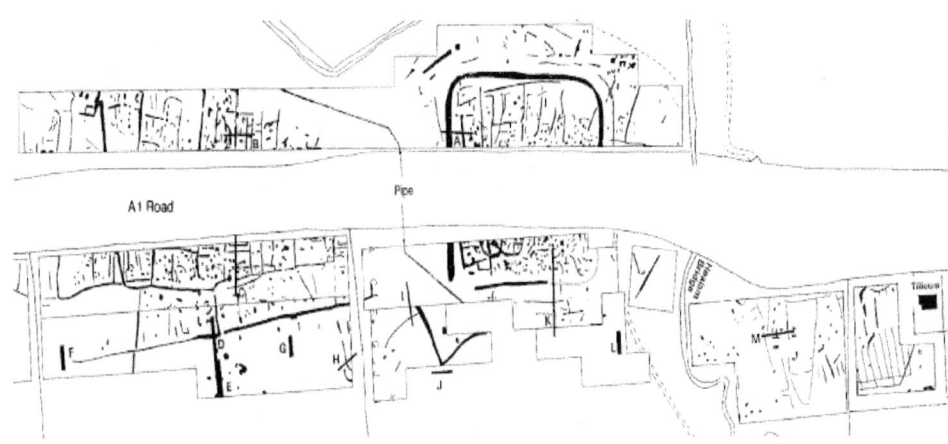

An early Flavian period fort has been found at Catterick and there are suggestions this was occupied either by the Ninth Legion or the fourth cohort of Gauls. Illustration #17 shows its location adjacent to the River Swale (Bidwell & Hodgson 2009, pp.141–145).

Illustration #17: Plan of the fort & Vicus at Catterick
(Bidwell & Hodgson 2009, p.144)

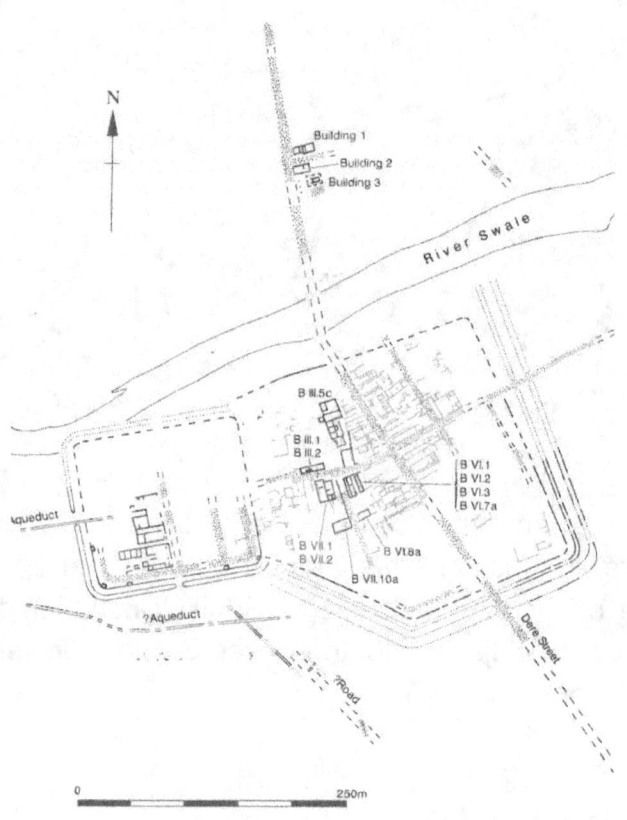

The roman fort at Old Carlisle which covers 4.4 acres has never been excavated. The plan (Illustration #18) of the fort and vicus has been created using aerial photographs. Small scale excavation on the vicus took place in 1956 and

2002 and shards of pottery dated to AD 2/3 have been found by a local farmer.

Illustration #18: Plan of Old Carlisle
(Bidwell & Hodgson 2009, p.125)

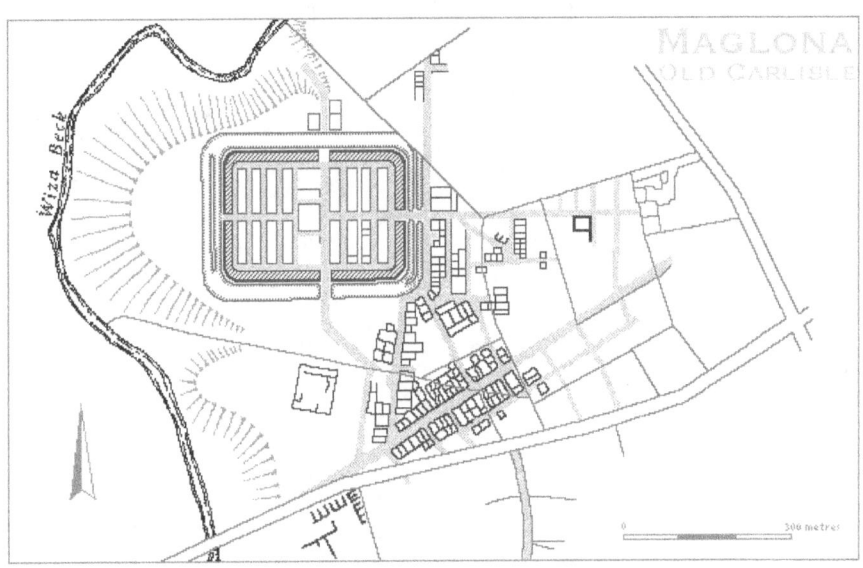

Scalesceugh is located east of the fort at Wreay and borders the west side of the road to Carlisle (5 miles away). Here the legionary tile and pottery kilns have been identified which produced tiles stamped with the Ninth Legion marks. Tiles and pottery have also been found at Carlisle and Stanwix. The site dates to the Trajanic period (Bidwell & Hodgson 2009, p.70).

The Roman fort at Carlisle has been identified using Ground Penetrating Radar (GPR) and lies partly buried beneath the superstructure of Carlisle Castle Keep as shown on Illustration #19. Tiles have been found here which are stamped with the Ninth legion and were made a Scalesceugh but no dateable material has been found.

Illustration #19: Plan of Carlisle
(Higham & Jones 1991)

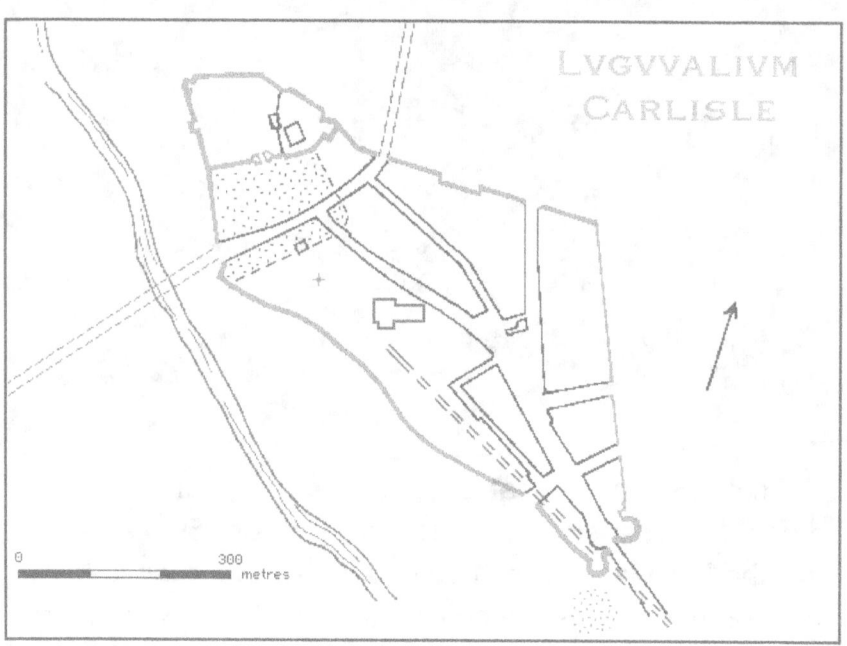

The fort at Stanwix may have been a vexilation fortress and hence may have been occupied by a detachment of the Ninth Legion; since a tile with the Legion's name on has been found at the fort.

7. Archaeological Sites around the World

Other than Britain, Zaragozza in Spain was for a time the retired veteran's camp of the Ninth Legion and two coins, dated to the late republic, and bearing the Legion's mark have been found there. From AD 9 - AD 43 the Ninth legion was stationed at Siscia in Pannonia Superior (Croatia), apart from a short period in Africa from AD 17 - AD 23 where they helped crush the revolts of Tacfarinas in the provinces of Mauretania and Africa. They returned to Siscia in AD 23.

Little is known about the fort since a second century roman town was built over it, followed by a medieval city and present day Sisak. We know that it was built in timber and the Ninth Legion's presence at Siscia is attested to by Strabo and Dio Cassius. A tombstone belonging to Lucius Valerius Proclus a member of the Ninth Legion was found at Nedan nearby ILS 2666b (Dessau 2009).

Two tombstones were found in Rome which belongs to Lucius Aemilius Carus, a military tribune of the Ninth legion and Tiberius Claudius Galianus Vitalis, an officer of the Ninth Legion.

The fort at Nijmegen has been excavated several times and the layout of the buildings occupied by the Ninth Legion are highlighted on Illustration #20. J.K Haalebos' excavations of 1960-63 found an altar and two brick fragments belonging to the Ninth Legion (Bishop 2013a, pp.91–94). The site has recently been re-excavated and the resultant dispute over dating is discussed later.

Illustration 20: Plan of the fort at Nijmegen
(Bishop 2013a, p.93)

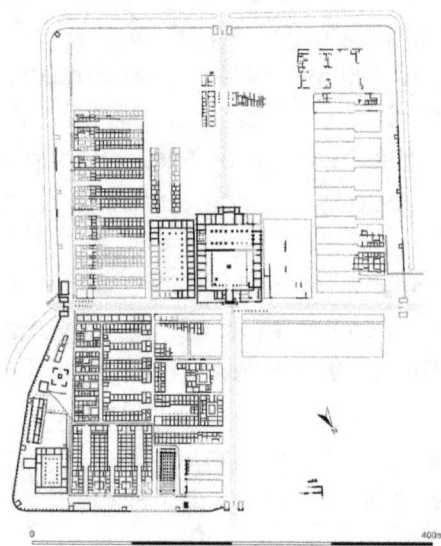

At Lambaesis, an inscription and tombstone have been found which is dedicated to Lucius. Novius Crispinus Martialis Saturninus, a military Tribune of the Ninth Legion. The tombstone has been dated to AD 150 when he died in office as governor of Africa (Bishop 2013a, pp.106–108). Illustration #21 shows the extent of the fort.

Illustration #21: Plan of the fort at Lambaesis
(Bishop 2013a, p.107)

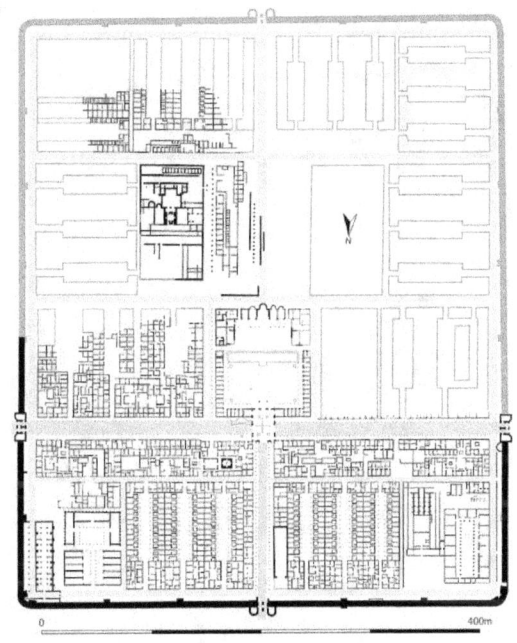

At Petra in Jordan the splendid mausoleum tomb of Lucius Aninius Sextus Florentinus, an ex legate of the Ninth Legion has been cited by Richmond (Richmond 1955) as evidence of the possibility that the Ninth Legion travelled from Britain to Judea. The site of the tomb is at location 12 on Illustration #22.

Illustration #22: Plan of Petra showing the location of the tomb of Lucius
Aninius Sextus Florentinus
(Browning 1989)

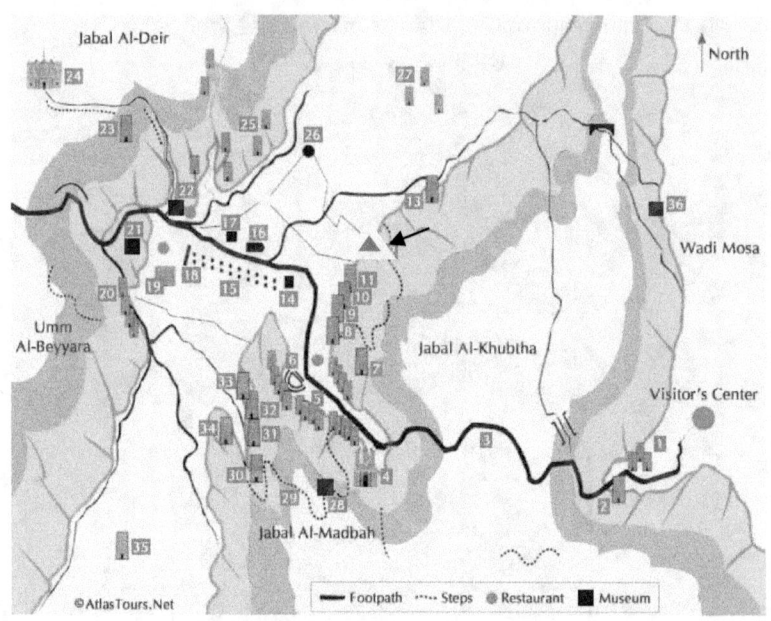

Part Three

8. The Disappearance of the Ninth

Much on the movement of Rome's military might northwards through the home counties and into present day Lincolnshire, Yorkshire and beyond, has not yet been fully documented, with some dates and events attributed being purely conjectural. The main local tribal grouping was the *Corieltauvi* though it is not known whether they surrendered to Rome after the invasion was underway or indeed resisted the invaders at any point in the campaign? History as recorded by several writers concentrates on the fighting further south against the *Catevellauni* and their allies, yet literary and archaeological record searches have produced no certain evidence either way.

As we have seen the Romans tried to establish and demonstrate a degree of control over the defeated tribes by placing forts to dominate important native centres, as for example at Colchester and possibly an early fort at Lincoln (probably at Down Hill). There is some additional evidence of a fort built at Ancaster (known for its Iron Age settlement) and aerial photographic evidence has revealed another fort at Owmby. There is, however, no evidence of a fort at Sleaford despite this being the most important *Corieltauvi* centre.

The push northwards sometime after the initial invasion, secured the Trent Valley and the Humber Estuary. This campaign was almost certainly spearheaded by the Ninth Legion with its attached *auxilia*. The early distribution of Roman military forces in the East Midlands was through a series of vexillation forts placed at several strategic points such as Longthorpe, Newton-on-Trent, Osmanthorpe, Rossington and most probably Kirmington, with (perhaps) Lincoln and possibly Ancaster. These dispositions served to control that broad swath of territory along the line of the Trent and up to the Humber. Additionally, there is a small, 1.8 acre, Roman fort at Marton of uncertain date; but this may well prove to be sited on another earlier fortification and not of Roman construction.

The greatest challenge facing Roman rule in the new province of Britannia occurred in AD 60/61 with the revolt of Boudicca and the Iceni tribe. Again neither the written sources nor the archaeological record provide any certainty on the attitude of the *Corieltauvi* to this revolt. It is widely accepted a large contingent of the Ninth Legion's cavalry and auxiliaries suffered a defeat at the hands of the rebels. This occurred while the Legion marched south to aid the besieged town of Colchester and the Ninth's cavalry alone escaped and subsequently forced to take refuge in a nearby fort (probably Longthorpe). There are however, no reasons to believe any part of the Ninth Legion's main force took part in the final battle that defeated Boudicca. It is more likely the surviving vexillations were used to maintain order in the East Midlands whilst the auxiliaries were reformed.

Clues in the Landscape:

At Lincoln we know of a Legionary fortress built during the reign of Nero (c.AD 61) and after the Boudicca revolt. Again, detailed information on the dates and extent of the Ninth legionary occupation at Lincoln isn't readily available. After the legionaries left, we know the Romans founded a colony on the site and, in the late first to early second century embarked on a major public works programme which saw the city thrive, spreading down to the Witham and along the roads north and south of the walled enclosure. During the later empire, Lincoln became a provincial capital and its fortifications were greatly improved, allowing the city to continue as a strong urban presence in the mid to late fourth century.

Roads and Waterways:

The main road system of Roman Lincolnshire has been well established for some time. Generally but not always fully metalled, the following roads formed the main lines of communications in the area. Ermine Street, Fosseway, King Street, Mareham Lane, Tillbridge Lane and Wragby Road, running to Ulceby Cross and then down through Burgh-le-Marsh. A branch route to the coast opposite a Roman site in Norfolk, is assumed to be the site of a ferry crossing of the Wash from Owmby to the Wolds There are other secondary routes recognised as probably being ancient track-ways that were used in the Roman period and may or may not have been metalled. Caistor High Street, Blue Stone Heath Road running from close to Ludford along the ridge towards Ulceby Cross, Barton Street. The road running along the edge of the marsh becoming Louth Street was probably not considered a major highway. The only Roman bridge hereabouts was been identified at Lincoln, where timbers were seen during work in the nineteenth century. There is some evidence for a ford existing across the Trent at Littleborough where Tillbridge Lane crosses the river. There is also evidence for a causeway across the Car Dyke at Billingborough.

Canals and Navigable Rivers:

The Foss Dyke is almost certainly Roman. It connects the navigable Witham to the Trent and would have allowed safe inland communication from the Wash (also via navigable rivers into East Anglia) to the Humber and thence to York. River transport was most likely by river boat rather than the heavier sea-going vessels; and cargo would have been trans-shipped at suitable points along the route. Possible hard standing sites have been identified at Lincoln and Fiskerton. Car Dyke is also Roman although the southern section in Lincolnshire was not navigable along its entire length and was most likely used as a catch-water drain to help the draining of the fen margin to assist settlement construction. The construction of the Car Dyke was certainly a major undertaking and associated with the visit of Hadrian in the early second century. The theory it was also associated with a planned extensive imperial estate located in the fens is still only conjecture.

Rural Settlement:

Major study work was carried out in the fens by Hallam (1964) and more recent work by the Fenland Survey has reinforced his findings. Second century settlement in the fens of Lincolnshire has traditionally been seen as being on virgin land as directed by the Imperial government (possibly for an Imperial estate?). Recent arguments tend to counter this by pointing out several Iron Age settlements have now been found in these areas. The draining of the fens does not necessarily need a central organization and the local community might have been expected to complete both drainage works and dykes to protect against floods. (EMRF Resource Assessment of Roman Lincolnshire). There was further work in the 1960's by the Welland Valley Research Committee on the Welland gravels investigating Romano-British settlements (Simpson 1966).

Most work has been done on likely Roman villas. However virtually all of this excavation was carried out in the eighteenth, nineteenth and early twentieth centuries. Winterton is the only large villa site to have enjoyed some recent, extensive excavation. This revealed the development of a Roman settlement and field system from the original Iron Age to the fourth century with late Roman reorganization then of a large farm or estate centre. The evidence from villa excavations in Lincolnshire tend to suggest these date from the later second century onwards into the fourth century. It's possible that the relatively early date of the majority of the excavations has created a bias against earlier Iron Age and Roman remains being there.

Archaeological techniques in the nineteenth century were not adequate enough to fully record the more ephemeral remains of huts and timber buildings. Also large scale rebuilding in stone would undoubtedly cause damage to earlier levels to a significant degree. There tends to be a perception that there are more villas in the south-west of the county (Hingley 1989, Fig.68) but these can be seen in some density running northwards along the Lincolnshire edge following the line of the escarpment. There are fewer in the Wolds and they are not found in the fenland although a late Roman high-status farmstead with hypocaust system and painted plaster was unearthed during work at West Deeping. There are other such sites awaiting excavation in this general area.

Some of the high status sites close to Lincoln might have been villas of a more suburban nature, built as retreats for rich officials or local magnates living and working in Lincoln. Once Lincoln becomes a provincial capital there would presumably have been an increase in the number government posts. Greetwell villa has late mosaics and was an extensive high status residence on a par with the grandest villas in Britain. (Another, near Brough north of the Humber may also be revealed to be of high value?).

A related issue when discussing Lincoln and its hinterland is the extent of the *territorium* of the colony though several authors have suggested differing boundaries, there is no certain evidence for the nature and extent of Lincoln's land holdings.

Any change in the nature of settlement from the Iron Age into the Roman period remains difficult to assess from the archaeological point of view; and how much change there is in material culture is still subject to debate. The spread of a cash economy and how coinage was distributed across a variety of settlements and settlement types cannot yet be accurately determined. It is said that Iron Age settlement continues virtually unchanged into the Roman period yet, there are marked differences in Roman settlement patterns later in the second, third and fourth centuries when compared to those of the Iron Age. True there is a variety of Romano-British settlements across the differing geology of Lincolnshire, yet the processes of these changes are still not completely understood.

Religion and Ritual:

Roman temples are known at Nettleton and Kirmington where votive offerings have been recorded. Altars and statuary are found at Lincoln where one would expect a high degree of religious activity as it was a Roman city from its foundation as a colony. Roman government was closely tied to religion. There was a sculptural tradition in Lincoln and at Ancaster which has a number of surviving religious sculptures. It is significant that both sites would have easy access to good quality stone. Other finds have suggested other religious centres including an altar from Whaplode, a ritual crown from Deeping St James and a votive tablet from Saltesford. A large cemetery was excavated at Ancaster with about three hundred bodies, the majority of which had been laid east-west. The cemetery is suggested as fourth century but awaits full determination.

Earlier cemeteries have been found at Lincoln. A number of early tombstones found south of the legionary fortress argue for this perhaps being associated with the presumed earlier fort. Recently, cremations have been found just west of the lower walled area of the city. Other cemeteries have been identified around the Roman city but for the most part they were noted during residential development in the last hundred years or so and have now been built over (East Midlands Archaeological Research Framework: Resource Assessment of Roman Lincolnshire).

Roman barrows are rare in the area although there may be more judging by cropmark evidence? Riseholme barrow and the barrows at Revesby have both been interpreted as Roman. Evidence for Christianity in Roman Lincolnshire is equally sparse. There are indications of Christian practice at Walesby, Bishop Norton and Caistor and of course burials at Ancaster. At Lincoln there is some evidence to support claims a Bishop from Lincoln attended the Council of Arles in AD 314 and the excavations at St Paul-in-the-Bail, Lincoln, tend to support the theory there was a Christian community present in Lincoln during the late Roman period.

Industry:

There are pottery kilns at Boultham/Swanpool near Lincoln. Several kilns have been identified but few excavated. The Trent valley industry comprises a number of kilns in Lea, Fenton/Torksey and Knaith (Field & Palmer-Brown 1991). South Carlton kilns are known to have supplied Hadrian's Wall, possibly using the Foss Dyke for their transportation north. There are a number of kilns in the area around Linwood and Market Rasen but again little excavation is recorded as with the kilns at Messingham, Roxby and Bourne.

Salterns exist in an arc around the edge of the fenland in Lincolnshire, at Ingoldmells and at Wrangle. These salterns lay on the salt marsh at the edge of the marshy land often with settlement nearer the sea on the more stable marshland. No Roman saltern has been fully excavated and the techniques used in salt production are not certain nor are the dates of production known. It is worth noting that areas of salt-working identified by Ptolemy and called Salinae in the territory of the *Catevellauni* and possibly located in Lincolnshire. Formerly identified as Droitwich a recently published reassessment of Ptolemy's map suggests these may be on the east coast of Lincolnshire perhaps on the now eroded coastal area beyond Ingoldmells (Strang 1997, 23).

Iron was produced and there are ironstone deposits suitable for production in the county; but the evidence for its use during Roman times is sketchy. There is however evidence for iron smelting at Hibaldstow, at Sapperton and at Creeton Quarry (Trimble 1995). The main commercial suburb of Lincoln shows evidence of iron-working and finds of slag are not uncommon on Roman sites. However, the evidence for industrial production sites along the limestone ridge has not been systematically recorded and survey work that has been done is limited and awaits publication.

There are also quarries at Lincoln and Ancaster however the continued industrial use of these quarries into the medieval, post-medieval and modern periods has made their examination and recording very difficult. There may also have been exploitation of gravel for roads.

Lincoln again has evidence of continued occupation by Rome well into the fifth century. There may also have been a Christian community there led by a bishop? On the Humber there is evidence for late Roman settlement in the late fourth century. A wide aisled building of the fourth century at Barton-on-Humber and a very late fourth century hoard provide an example of a farmstead surviving into the late fourth and perhaps even the early fifth centuries. Evidence assessed for the south Humber bank points to a fair amount of late Roman occupation (Whitwell 1988).

Evidence from other parts of the county is varied. Anglo-Saxon burials are found in and adjacent to Roman villas like those at Scampton and Denton where an inhumation was found in the centre of a mosaic, evidence that the rooms of a Roman building were at least recognisable at the time of the burial. In the fens some sites with Anglo-Saxon pottery have now been found but they are not normally on the same site as Roman pottery, suggesting that rising waters had affected late Roman settlement.

A study of early Germanic metalwork and the fifth century cemeteries in the north of the county as at Kirton-in-Lindsey and Elsham has lead to the suggestion that there might have been Germanic mercenaries settled in North Lincolnshire before the end of the Roman period (Leahy 1984 & 1993). At Hibaldstow there are possible building platforms over fourth century building remains, indicating later occupation of the site possibly into the fifth century. There is further evidence at Sapperton for fifth century occupation in one of the buildings excavated but all evidence points to a general gradual decline and decay of most Roman settlements.

There are many other areas of interest in the time frame pertaining to the presence of the Ninth Legion and beyond but space here has not allowed for their inclusion. Also, further work on the coasts of Lincolnshire, East Yorkshire and Berwick would be useful. Basic surveys and excavations are still needed to record information in these areas which could then be incorporated into existing databases and placed in the public domain. Such data would help support or refute much conjecture – and is desperately overdue.

And into the mist:

On the 7th of October 1854 an article in the York Herald reported that workmen putting in new drainage, had found 'a very interesting stone' during their excavations. This turned out to be a building inscription (See page 25) created by the Ninth Legion and dated AD 107-108 (RIB 665). This was not the first recorded interest in the story of the Ninth Legion as John Horsley, writing in 1732 in his *'Roman Antiquaries of Britain'* recorded that it 'might possibly be broke or incorporated with the Legio Sexta Victrix' which was based on a (RIB 2462.17) brick stamp reading Legio Nona Victrix found in York in 1715 (Horsley 1732). In 1835, Count Borghesi proposed a scenario where the Ninth Legion were finally overwhelmed in a rebellion and were subsequently replaced by the Sixth legion (Campbell 2013). T. Mommsen in *'Römische Geschichte'* (1885) similarly suggests the Ninth were attacked at their fortress of York and annihilated soon after AD 108 during a revolt of the northern tribes led by the Brigantes (Mommsen 1885). Mommsen also put forward the theory of a 'British' war due to Hadrian's biographer who tells us that the 'Britons could not be kept under Roman control' and (Fronto 2012) in a letter to Marcus Aurelius written in AD 162 providing advice about the Parthian war, reminds the emperor that 'under the rule of your grandfather Hadrian, what great numbers of soldiers were slain by the Jews and what a number by the Britons'.

Emil Ritterling, in his survey of legions (1925) proposed that by AD 119 the Ninth Legion had probably already met its fate - or by AD 125 at the very latest - as by then Hadrian had restored the province's army back to four legions by deploying the Sixth in AD 122 - albeit for a short time only (Ritterling 1925). Professor Wilhelm Weber in 1936 took a similar view when he found an inscription belonging to Titus Pontus Sabinus (CIL 5829/ILS 2726) which mentioned a British 'expedition' identified by Weber as in AD 119 or AD 122. He suggested the Ninth Legion was finally destroyed at York, probably in AD 119 and the rebellion was finally subdued by the Sixth Legion (Weber 1936). Similarly, in

1928, H M D Parker in his book *'The Roman Legions'* (Parker 1994) stated the ninth legion were unable to cope with a British revolt and were destroyed not later than AD 122. E B Birley however introduced a dissenting voice in 1948. In the Durham University journal he wrote a paper called *'Britain after Agricola and the end of the Ninth Legion'*, where he suggested the Legion was transferred out of Britain by Trajan in connection with the Parthian war of AD 114-116 and the Sixth Legion was then brought over to supplement the garrison during building work on Hadrian's wall (Birley 1948). Surprisingly, Sir Ian Richmond in *'Roman Britain'* 1955 declared it to be 'without doubt' that the Ninth Legion was cashiered by Hadrian and, given his eminent position as Head of the British Museum, this held considerable sway despite there being no evidence to support his assertion (Richmond 1955).

Later, Winston Churchill in his *'A History of the English-Speaking Peoples'*, having taken into account the views of eminent scholars, reassuringly supported the 'pre Richmond' position writing that the unit had disappeared 'in combating an obscure rising of the tribes in Northern Britain' (Churchill 1956). At about the same time and possibly as a reaction to Sutcliff's fictional account, other theories started to emerge many of which featured the newly excavated site at Nijmegen (Holland). Stanier, despite vehement opposition (Stanier 1965) continued to insist that there was no evidence to suggest the Ninth Legion had ever left Britain. .

Nijmegen:

J E Bogaers was surprised to find artefacts belonging to the Ninth Legion at Nijmegen in 1967. In his book co-authored with Haalebos in 1979, he states the Ninth Legion occupied Nijmegen from c.AD 121-130 and that the tile, mortarium fragment and altar found at Aachen support this. The Legion was then posted to Judea where it was destroyed in the Bar Kokhba revolt. They also proposed the Ninth Legion was initially moved to Nijmegen to rest and regroup after being mauled in Britain in AD 121 (Bogaers & Haalebos 1979). J P Sijpesteijn excavated nearby at E-wijk from 1961-70 and a phalera stamped with LEG IX HISP was found by a metal detectorist. Sijpesteijn suggested this was a part of a cavalryman's or officer's harness brought from England by its owner and lost in Holland (Sijpesteijn 1996).

Bogaers has suggested that the whole legion was present at Nijmegen and not just a vexilation of two cohorts commanded by a camp prefect? Furthermore he proposes the presence of an unnamed tribune of the Ninth Legion at Tier in Germany proves this (CIL, 13, 4030) (Alföldy & Preussische Akademie der Wissenschaften 1995). Haalebos suggested (Bogaers & Haalebos 1979) the camp prefect Latinius Macer who dedicated the altar at Aachen was on a special assignment, perhaps preparing the departure for Judea or in command of a detachment at Nijmegen. Birley has refuted this on the grounds that given the unrest,

Hadrian would not have been in a position to release a whole Legion from Britain at that time (Birley 1971). In the absence of an inscription or tombstone connected with the Legate or Aquilifer there is no evidence to support the whole Legion being there. Later Haalebos in his *'Roman troops in Nijmegen'* continues to argue that the Ninth Legion occupied the fort at Nijmegen from AD 122-130 AD before moving to Judea; but revises his view to suggest that the Legion survived there and were subsequently lost in Parthia in AD 161 (Haalebos 2000).

Dando-Collins (2010) puts forward the proposal that other authors use Nijmegen to 'scotch the Britain theory and advance destruction in the orient', although he concedes that two cohorts of the Ninth Legion may have been there from AD 113 to 116 under the command of the camp prefect and that they probably returned to Britain in AD 116 and re-joined the Legion. Russell (2011) expresses doubts as to the reliability of the initial dating for Nijmegen and states the 'evidence of the theory of strategic transfer of the Ninth being taken out of Britain rather than dying here, is rather flimsy'. Interestingly, Driessen (2009) in the early Flavian castra and the Flavian-Trajanic stone legionary fortress at Nijmegen records the re-examination of Haalebos' trenches and revises dating of the stratigraphy using wooden material dateable to the mid AD 80's to early 90's. He also found a coin of Domitian which was dated to AD 83 which depicted an Aquila flanged by Signums and LEG VIIII underneath.

During the 1970's it was presumed the German legions were sent to Trajan's Parthian war of 114-116AD and the Ninth Legion was stationed at Nijmegen to replace them. Nesselhauf for example, argued that the Legion replaced the 10th Gemina in AD 114 and was there until AD 119 (Birley 1971, p.75). In contrast, Keppie has argued that they were stationed at Nijmegen during the Dacian war of AD 105-108 and the Ninth Legion was later replaced at Nijmegen by vexilations of three other legions (VI, XXII 7 XXX) in AD 107 (1998). He is doubtful that the whole Legion transferred to Nijmegen during Hadrian's reign but is of the firm opinion there is no credible evidence for the Ninth Legion being lost in Britain. Salway (1993) takes the Nijmegen theory further and suggests the Ninth Legion were moved to the Rhine frontier and destroyed in Germany during AD 120-125. An inscription from Tivoli, Italy (ILS 1025) (Dessau 2009) reveals that Lucius Roscius Aelianus Maecius Celer was a military tribune in 'Legion IX Hispana, and also of a detachment of that Legion in the German Campaign'. Both Birley (1981) and Burn (1969) believe, on the grounds that the emperor's name is omitted, that it is most likely that the 'German Campaign' is from Domitian's Chatian war of 83AD. (Domitian was declared Damnatio memoriae.)

Judea:

Mattingly (cited in Campbell 2013), suggests in his agreement with Haalebos' original theory, the Ninth Legion was transferred from Britain to Nijmegen and destroyed during the Bar Kokhba revolt (AD 132–136). Goldsworthy (2011) suggested the same fate as does the classicist G R Watson in his book *'The Roman Soldier'* (1969) writing that 'the loss of the IX Hispana was probably during the Jewish war of 132-5'. Campbell (2013) takes the same view whilst A R Birley suggests that involvement in the Jewish war is likely if the evidence from Nijmegen is dated correctly. However, he is sceptical that this is the case. Mor initially supports the Judea theory but later, Mor (1986) argues that the Ninth Legion must have been destroyed or annihilated by AD 126 at the latest and hence could not have been in Judea as the dates do not tally. He believes, as does Stanier (1965) that the Legion which perished in Judea was the Twenty Second Deiotariana, already stationed there. Russell (2011), similarly dismissive of the theory, suggests it 'stretches the evidence beyond all credibility'.

Parthia:

Watson suggests that the Ninth Legion was destroyed in Armenia around AD 161. Salway (1993) too states they were destroyed in AD 161 in the Middle East whereas Campbell (2013) agreeing with Watson, reckons they were annihilated in AD 161 in Armenia at Elegeia under Severianus where they were all killed by a continuous arrow storm. In Rome a military inscription was found (ILS2288) on a pillar which has been dated to c.AD 165 which lists thirty three legions and the Ninth legion is among them? Yet another list from AD 108 has the ninth legion present (2013a, p.9).

The logical conclusion is the Ninth must have been destroyed sometime between AD 108 and AD165 has been used by scholars to support the Parthian theory. Haalebos also cites a military diploma from the province of Moesia dated to 161AD which mentions a Q Numisius as a consul and suggests that he (CIL, 11, 5760) (Alföldy & Preussische Akademie der Wissenschaften 1995) and Quintus Lemidias Numisius, Junior military tribune of the Ninth Spanish Legion are the same people and hence must have been a tribune c.AD 140. However Birley (1981, pp.254–6) suggests that the consul was actually the son of a tribune of the Ninth Legion and that the tribune served with the Ninth Legion in the early Ad 120's.

Nisher has suggested that in AD 161 a newly founded legion which had not yet seen action was destroyed in Parthia (Birley 1971, p.74). Mor (1986) vehemently argues that the Ninth was not lost in Parthia due to the fact that all officers whose tombstones or inscriptions have been found had retired or died before AD 140 - some 21 years before the Parthian conflict started. Birley (1981) is of the opinion that there is no evidence of the Ninth Legion having been in Parthia - a view supported by (Russell 2010) who argues that being 'cut to pieces in the east is mere supposition'. Finally, Dando-Collins (2010) indicates that it was not the Ninth which was butchered in Parthia but elements of the Sixth Ferrata and the Tenth Fretensis legions who were stationed there.

9. Supposition

Plague in the East:

Sicker (2000) in his book *'The Pre Islamic Middle East'* suggests a plague that swept through the armies of the eastern provinces in AD 165 was the cause of the disappearance of the Ninth Legion. However, as Mor argued in relation to Parthia, by then all the known officers of the Ninth Legion for whom tombstones survive had already died or at least retired and hence it is very unlikely that this was the cause of the Legion's demise.

Resurgence of Britain – or a British War:

Russell (2010, p.183) has recently supported the 'British War' theory (first put forward by Mommsen) by reiterating the evidence from the *Scriptores Histroriae Augustae* that the Romans could not keep the British under their control and suggests this may have involved a major uprising in the frontier zone of Northern Britain. The same anonymous document tells us that in AD 122 Hadrian came to Britain to 'correct many faults within the province and to build a wall eighty miles long, to separate the Romans and the barbarians'. This suggests that either a major revolt, issues with discipline in the ranks, or a major military disaster had already taken place, any of which could have involved the Ninth Legion. There has in fact, always been that belief among archaeologists in the theory of a demise in Britain but, like that of Stanier before them; their work was to some extent overlooked or at least attracted less attention than the Nijmegen based alternatives. It is perhaps appropriate to re visit some of this work now.

The Reign of Trajan:

Morrison states the Ninth Legion was annihilated during the revolt of the Brigantes perhaps AD 115-7 (Birley 1981). Birley (1971) extolls the view that they removed to Carlisle to build fortifications along Stanegate frontier and that the Sixth Victrix were moved to York to bring the garrison back up to four legions. With the Ninth possibly suffering heavy casualties at the hands of the Carvetti. (ILS 2656) he records Lucius Valerius Proculus bringng more reinforcements to Britain during Trajan's reign and the title given to Trajan dates that event to between AD 108 and 110 suggesting regular military engagements continued in Britain between AD 108 and 117.

The Reign of Hadrian:

Brian Hartley examines whether the Legion was present at Carlisle during the early years of Hadrian's reign and cites evidence from Scalesceugh where tiles were produced by the Ninth and which have been found nearby at Carlisle, Old Carlisle and Stanwix in Cumbria. The tiles at these sites are all stamped LEG VIIII HISP. The 1997 excavations at Vindolanda (Birley et al. 1998, pp.62–65) by Robin Birley et al., included the discovery of a tombstone dedicated to a cavalry commander who previously served with the Ninth Legion and died in a British war. Subsequent examination in great detail, including restoring the section shown in square brackets, the translation reads:

To the spirits of the departed: Titus Ann[ius, son of -, in the --voting-district, *(cognomen)*, from (town), Centurion of (legion 9, Hisp, acting-commander of the Ist Cohort] of Tungrians [a thousand strong; aged --years, with --years service:] died-in-the[...] war. killed [by the Britons. Titus Ann(ius ---)] his son and Arc (?) [his wife, or his freedman], his heirs, had this errected (in accordance with his testament).

In AD 122 Hadrian Aulius Plautius Nepos (the new Governor of Britain) with the Sixth Legion and vexilations from three other legions arrived in the province to put down an uprising and to stabilise the northern frontier by building a wall eighty Roman miles long. The Sixth Legion were moved to the fortress at York suggesting the Ninth were no longer there (Salway 1993). Russell (2010) has argued that most people forget historical sources pointing out that a large amount of troops were lost in Britain at the same time as troops were lost in other provinces. Mattingly (2007, p.90) looked at the numismatic evidence from the reign of Hadrian and concluded the two coins which depicted Britannia on the reverse date to AD 119 and 122 commemorated victories over the British, or at least the restoration of peace after revolts in the province. Stanier also supports this view. During the early AD 120's, in northern England, Malton, Aldborough, Slack, Catterick and Chester-le-Street forts were all burnt and London set ablaze. A statue of Hadrian was violently decapitated and thrown into the River Thames which suggests that the province was in open revolt (Jarrett 1976).

Jarrett also noticed military diplomas, found throughout the Empire relate to the retirement of thirteen cavalry and around thirty seven auxiliary cohorts in Britain during the early years of Hadrian's reign. This act alone would have left the legion short of manpower and the northern tribes could well have seized their advantage with Rome's numerical weakness apparent.

Mor (1986) has proposed that the Ninth Legion did in fact disappear during the reign of Hadrian 'at the sword points of the Brigantes'. Stanier (1965) made a number of interesting observations about how the Legion's close links with the local people may also have impacted on their fate? These assertions are explored more fully later. (Dando-Collins 2010) notes at the same time the Ninth Legion disappears from Britain, in AD 122 five auxiliary cohorts also disappear which includes one mixed cavalry and infantry cohort. This is the exact amount of auxiliaries which a legion would usually take on campaign and hence it is reasonable that they may have met their fate together. He also suggests they were lured into a trap in Scotland and butchered by a confederation of northern tribes and the direct consequence of this was the building of Hadrian's Wall. Finally, Stevens (1966) argues the Ninth were destroyed in AD 125 in a British conflict.

Hadrian's Wall:

Stanier (1965) suggests when the Legion was based at Carlisle they were heavily involved in building the western section of Hadrian's Wall, which was built using timber and turf due to a scarcity of stone and suitable quarry sites. He goes on to say that when the northern tribes became aware of the building work, they attacked the Ninth Legion at Carlisle and massacred it. Ramm (1978) argues that the Legion was moved to Carlisle post AD 108 and was involved in building the wall. A R Birley puts forward a similar opinion and notes that inscriptions have been found from the wooden wall with names of centuries who built it but as yet no legion due to the poor preservation. Stevens (1966) has argued that the Ninth legion built sections of Hadrian's Wall and that the wall was started as part of a 'Trajanic withdrawal and not a Hadrianic defeat, of a legion'. He goes on to argue the legion was destroyed in a second British war in AD 125.

Part Four

Structure & Command:

Because Roman legions were not standing units until the Marian reforms (c.107 BC), and were instead created as necessary, used as required then disbanded again, several hundred legions were named and numbered throughout Roman history. To date, only about fifty have been identified. In the time of the Early Roman Empire, it is believed at any one time, there were usually about twenty five to thirty five permanent legions.

A legion consisted of several cohorts of heavy infantry known as legionaries. It was almost always accompanied by one or more units of fighting auxiliaries. Apart from their commanders, these were not Roman citizens but provided the cavalry, scouting troops and skirmishers needed to complement the legion's heavy infantry. The recruitment of non-citizens was rare at first but appears to have become common in times of great need. Caesar appears to have recruited one, the Legio V Alaudae mostly from non-citizen Gauls.

The size of a typical legion varied throughout the history of ancient Rome, with complements of 4,200 legionaries and 300 equites drawn from the wealthier classes. In early Rome all troops provided their own equipment; and in the republican period of Rome, the infantry were split into ten cohorts, each of four maniples of one hundred and twenty legionaries. 5,200 men plus auxiliaries were recruited in the imperial period, split into ten cohorts, nine of 480 men each, plus the 'first' cohort holding 800 men.

In the Republic, legions had an ephemeral existence. Except for Legio I to IV, which were the consular armies (two per consul) other units were levied by campaign. Rome's Italian allies were also required to provide a legion equivalent to support each Roman Legion. In the middle term of the Republic, legions were composed of the following units:

Equites (cavalry): Originally the most prestigious unit; and where wealthy young Roman men displayed their skill and prowess. This lay the foundation for an eventual political career. Cavalry equipment was purchased by each of the cavalrymen and consisted of a round shield, helmet, body armour, sword and one or more spears or lances. The cavalry was outnumbered in the legion. In a total of roughly 3000 men, (plus the velites that normally enlarged the number to about 4200), the legion had only around 300 horsemen, divided into ten units of 30 men. These men were commanded by decurions. In addition to heavy cavalry, there would be the light cavalry, levied from poor citizens and wealthy young citizens not old enough to be in the hastati or the equites. In battle, they were used to disrupt and outflank enemy infantry formations and to fight off any enemy cavalry.

In the latter type of engagement they would often (though not always) dismount and fight a stationary battle on foot, an unusual tactic for the time, but one that offered significant advantages in stability and agility in a time before the introduction of stirrups.

Velites (light infantry): Mainly poorer citizens who could not afford to equip themselves properly. Their primary function was to act as skirmishers or spear-throwers who would engage the enemy early in order either to harass them or to cover the movement of troops behind them. After throwing their spears they would retreat through the gaps between the maniples, screened from the attack of the enemy by the heavy infantry lines. With the shortage of cavalry in the army of the early to mid-Republican period, the Velites were also used as scouts. They did not have a precise formal organization or formation.

Heavy infantry: This was the principal unit of the legion. The heavy infantry was composed of citizen legionaries that could afford the equipment composed of an iron helmet, shield, armour and pilum, a heavy javelin whose range was about thirty metres. After 387 BC, the preferred weapon for the Hastati and Principes was the gladius, an effective short sword. Their hobnailed sandals too (caligae) were found to be an effective weapon against a fallen enemy. Prior to the Marian reforms (see below), heavy infantry was subdivided, according to battle experience, into three separate lines.

The Hastati (*sing.* hastatus) usually consisted of raw or inexperienced soldiers, considered to be less reliable than legionaries of several years' service.

The Principes (*sing.* princeps): These were men in their prime (late twenties to early thirties). The Triarii (*sing.* triarius) were the veteran soldiers, who were to be used in battle only in extreme situations. They customarily rested on one knee when not engaged in combat. The Triarii served primarily as reserves designed to backstop the Hastati and Principes and were equipped with long hastae (spears) rather than the pilum and gladius. The Hastati and Principes stopped using spears in 387 BC. Armed with shield and sword, they fought in a phalanx formation. The sight of an advancing armoured formation of Triarii legionaries frequently served to discourage enemy troops in pursuit of retreating Hastati and Principes troops. *'Ad triarios redisse'* - To fall back upon the Triarii was a Roman idiom – meaning to use one's last resort.

Each of these three lines was then subdivided into chief tactical units called maniples. A maniple consisted of two centuries and was commanded by the senior of the two centurions. At this time, each century of Hastati and Principes consisted of 60 men; a century of triarii was 30 men. These 3000 men or twenty maniples of 120 men plus ten maniples of 60 men, together with about 1200 velites and 300 cavalry gave the mid Republican legion a nominal strength of about 4500 men.

Officers of the Ninth:

Russell (2010) has proposed that the Legion was 'savagely annihilated and that too few survived to allow it to be reformed'. He goes on to point out that three survivors at least are known to have been alive in AD 120-23. Birley (1981) discussed the careers of these survivors plus three other individuals from the Ninth Legion who are important to the debate. These were Aninius Sextius Florentinus, Lucius Barbuleius Ligarianus; Lucius Novius Crispinus Martialis Saturninus; Quintus Lemidias Numisius Junior; Lucius Aemilius Carus and Lucius Stertinius Noricus. In the 1830's, the Italian count Bartolomeo Borghesi began looking into the fledgling science of prosopography with regards to the Ninth Legion. He found an inscription at Minturno (CIL X 6006/ILS 1066): Lucius Barbuleius Ligarianus a Tribune Laticlavius (Senaorial Tribune) of the Ninth Spanish Legion (Birley 1981, pp.271–2). Lucius was a consul in AD 135. Therefore he was a tribune twenty years earlier from AD 113-115 during the reign of Trajan, meaning that the Legion was in existence after AD 108. A tombstone found at Miseno in Italy by Borghesi (CIL 10 1769) belongs to Aelius Asclepiades a native of Cilicia (modern day Turkey) and a soldier of the Ninth Victorius Legion who died aged 42 after eight years of service. Birley and Bogaers both found it significant that the man had Hadrian's family name Aelius and suggested that he enlisted in his native Cilicia. Keppie (1998) has suggested that he may have taken it on enlistment into the legions in

Miseno after leaving the fleet and hence served with the Ninth Legion during the reign of Hadrian. Borghesi found another inscription (CIL 6 1333 /ILS 1077) on a tombstone at Rome belonging to Lucius Aemilius Carus, military tribune of the Ninth Spanish Legion (Birley 1981, pp.274–5). Ritterling (1925) suggested a date of post AD 120 or possibly AD 122 for Carus' service in the Ninth Legion.

An inscription (CIL 8, 5355) (Birley 1981, p.271) found at Guelma, Algeria, which mentions a Lucius Stertinius Noricus a tribune of the Ninth Spanish Legion who served in Britain during the reign of Trajan and was recorded on a census late in the reign of Trajan in Britain, is dated to AD 114 due to the titles of the emperor on the inscription (ILS 1338).

Ritterling (1925) pointed out that the careers of certain officers 'seemed to have peaked too late for their service in the Ninth Legion to be restricted to the Trajanic period'. He concluded the Legion must have survived into the early years of Hadrian's reign at least. An inscription found at Lambaesis in Algeria (ILS 1070/CIL 8 2747) mentioned Lucius Novius Crispinus Martialis Saturninus military tribune of the Ninth Spanish legion and from that inscription, Ritterling suggested he had not served with the Ninth Legion until AD 123 and that the legion was not destroyed in a British war in AD 119 but in a second British war in the AD 120's (Ritterling 1925). Birley (1981, pp.276–7) suggested that the same individual served with the Ninth Legion in AD 124/5 but was not consul until AD 149/50 which is a career retardation of either twenty five or twenty six years. It proves he must have been a tribune of the Ninth Legion at the time when (as is being proposed) they were destroyed or annihilated in Britain.

At Petra a tombstone was found inside a mausoleum (CIL, 3 87 + 1414810) dedicated to Lucius Aninius Sextius Florentinus ex-legate of the Ninth Spanish Legion and Governor of Arabia. In 1960, we learnt that his period as Governor of Arabia was in AD 127/8 due to the Cave of Letters; hence he would have commanded the legion some five years earlier in AD 122/3. (Birley 1981, pp.237–9) suggested that he commanded the ninth legion during the early years of Hadrian's reign and was legate from AD 117/118-122/3. The German classicist Warner Eck has argued an inscription found at Attiggio, Umbria, Italy (CIL, 11, 5760) to Quintus Lemidias Numisius Junior, military tribune of the Ninth Spanish legion in AD 119, revealed he was a consul in AD 161 aged sixty years and hence seemed to have suffered a forty year retardation in his career. (Mor 1986) mentions an inscription from Industria (Turin), Italy which describes Marcus Cocceius Severus, a primus pilus of the Ninth Legion which Dobson (1978, p.260) has dated to AD 126. His career too suffered a retardation due to his next posting being in AD 140 and hence it is likely he was present when the Ninth met its fate.

The presence in Britain of three consecutive holders of the post of Tribune Laticlavius for the Ninth, Crispinus AD 117/9, Carus AD 119-21 and Saturninus AD 121/2, shows convincingly that the Legion continued into the AD 120s. With regard to Saturninus we know that he did not receive another posting until AD 147 when he was made consul and that his career went through a twenty five year retardation whereas Corus's career shows no retardation and continuous postings, which led to Jarrett (1976) suggesting that Saturninus was present at the destruction of the Legion in Britain but may have escaped on horseback just as Cerialis did during the Boudican revolt (Tacitus). We know that officers of the Roman Army have suffered retardation of their careers following severe military defeats as identified by Dando-Collins (2010) in relation to Martialis Valens who, in AD 51, lost nearly four thousand men to the Silures whilst commander of the Twentieth Legion in Wales. He then had a gap of almost seventeen years without another posting until AD 68. Similar examples exist from other parts of the empire.

Discussion: What happened to the Ninth:

It is clear the known archaeology relating to the Ninth Legion has been subject to numerous and very different interpretations and that there remains some significant disagreement between several eminent and experienced archaeologists as to what really happened to the Legion. In these circumstances - and in attempting to address this key question, it seems wise to begin with evidence rather than opinion and to review what is actually fact. It is known from the archaeology the Ninth arrived in Britain in AD 43 and moved North to York (via Longthorpe and Lincoln) arriving there by AD 71 at the latest. An inscription places the Legion in York in AD 107/8. There is no dateable evidence which places the Legion in Britain after that date.

There is evidence uncovered during the 1960's which has previously been used to place the Ninth Legion in Nijmegen between AD 121 and AD 130. However this has recently been reinterpreted by Driessen (2009) who re-excavated an area previously explored by Haalebos using more modern techniques. The latter had used the technique of excavating between bulks which is now much discredited because of problems accurately interpreting the stratigraphy and/or missing finds in the undisturbed areas of earthen surrounds. Driessen cleared the whole site to at least the original depth (sometimes lower) and uncovered wooden building posts belonging to a barrack block (at the same depth as the finds from the Ninth) which have been dendrodated to between the mid AD 80's and the early AD 90's. A Domitian coin from AD 83 was also discovered here.

There is, therefore, fairly convincing evidence that the Ninth or part of it was present in Nijmegen in the latter part of the first century AD. This is supported by accounts from Tacitus' Agricola and from an inscription describing the Ninth being in Germany in AD 83, and by further accounts from Tacitus and Dio Cassius recording the Legion's return. There is also the dedication by a Camp Prefect of the Ninth Legion of the altar to Apollo at Aachen (within a day's ride of Nijmegen). He died in AD 104 so could feasibly have commanded a vexilation of the Ninth Legion at Nijmegen in the latter part of the first century. However, there is no evidence this was one of the Ninth's last postings or that the Legion returned to Nijmegen at a later date.

Those archaeologists who proposed Judea in AD131/2 - 135 during the Bar Kokhba revolt as the likely place where the Ninth met its end, were building on the belief the Ninth had been in Nijmegen in AD 132 and transferred from there; but this is not supported by any evidence. There is no evidence from Tombstones, literature or other finds which support the view that the Legion was posted to fight in Judea. However there is literary evidence and a famous inscription from the entrance gates of Jerusalem which shows that Twenty Second Deiotariana were based there when the revolt began and that they too, were never heard of again. This led Mor to take the view that it was the Twenty Second and not the Ninth which perished in Judea.

The Parthian war, of AD 161-166, is known from literary evidence to have resulted in the annihilation of an entire Roman legion. However there is no evidence that the Ninth Legion was still in existence at that date. In fact the latest evidence from tombstones which relates to an officer with previous service in the Ninth, commemorates an individual who died in Lambaesis in modern day Algeria in AD 140 some twenty years before the Parthian war. The only evidence available from tombstones for individuals with any service in the Ninth and who appear to have been posted to Arabia, were for those based there in the mid AD 120's who were by then occupying senior administrative posts and not military ones. Dando–Collins suggests that the Sixth Ferrata and the Tenth Fretensis Legions were lost in the Parthian war; but again there is certainly no credible evidence it was the Ninth Legion!

This leaves us with evidence for the Ninth as definitely being retained in Britain in AD 107/8 with no evidence of a posting elsewhere, even at a later date. Evidence from the tombstone and inscription in Petra relating to Aninius Sextius Florentinus places him as Legate of the Ninth in approximately AD 122, although there is no indication of geographical location. This is where direct evidence runs out and some interpretation or inference is needed. Aninus moved from that post on promotion to be governor of Narbonne and then governor of Arabia where he died in AD 127. Given there was no retardation in his career, it seems likely he left the Ninth before the Legion failed in any way; but also confirms the Ninth still existed in the early AD 120s.

There is of course ceramic evidence of the Ninth in a number of locations around Carlisle. This cannot be dated but would be consistent with the whole legion being based there and in some nearby forts. It is known from literature (Dio Cassius and Suetonius) and from an inscription in Jarrow, that Quintus Pompeius Falco (who was governor of Britain before Nepos took over in AD 122) pushed on northwards during his reign and among others, Auxiliaries from Catterick moved north to Corbridge. It is therefore feasible that the Ninth moved up to Carlisle during AD 110's or 120's.

It is also known from literature and epigraphic evidence there were a number of periods of unrest in Britain in AD 115,117,119 and possibly AD 121/2. It also appears that with the exception of one attack on London, these troubles were largely confined to the north There are in support, a large number of tombstones of auxiliaries from this period. The Ninth Legion was the northernmost legion in Britain and would therefore have been sent to deal with any uprising north of York. Certainly by AD 122 the Sixth Legion is known to have arrived in York and there is no mention of the Ninth being there at that time.

It would seem from tombstone evidence that something drastic happened to the Ninth between AD 122 and AD 125 because a number of officers have those documented retardations in their careers, varying from twelve to twenty five years (or more) and all seem to date from the early AD 120's. This raises the possibility of an uprising north of the Stanegate frontier and the Ninth being sent out to deal with it but suffering some terrible defeat. Some officers may have escaped on horseback and later being punished for not remaining with their men. This was the case when Martialis Valens, a Legate of the Twentieth Valeria Victrix who survived an attack by the Silures in AD 51 when almost four thousand legionaries died and of course, there are similar parallels from the Teutenburg Forest disaster – but we digress.

Stanier (1965) has pointed out that the Ninth Legion had been stationed in York for a long period, meaning that as the years progressed their recruitment would have been mostly from the Brigantes tribe or their allies the Parisi of East Yorkshire or the Carvetti of Cumbria. Many legionaries had also intermarried with northern tribes. The Stanegate frontier bisected the territory of the Brigantes; and he suggests news of Hadrian's intention to build a wall splitting their lands in two may have been the catalyst for some catastrophic revolt? Alternatively, he proposes the slow progress of Romanisation in northern Britain meant the Legion could possibly have been more loyal to the local tribes than to Rome and there could have been a period of significant desertions from the Legion with legionaries being unwilling to kill their own tribes-people or extended families. Those officers who remained loyal might then have been punished with career retardation for failing to control the men under their command.

Either of these scenarios may explain the disappearance of the Ninth but the fact remains, there is no solid evidence that either is correct. The reality is a reliable answer to this tantalizing question will have to await the emergence of further archaeological evidence and, for the time being at least, the unknown fate of the Ninth remains just that.

Summary & Conclusion:

From the outset this was intended as an independent, non-academic research project with the aims of collating archaeological and historical evidence relating to the Ninth Legion, analysing and interpreting both to aid some general understanding of its eventual demise. To a large extent I feel this has been achieved. Known archaeology is described in the main body of the report and where possible, digital images of the artefacts have been used in support.

Evidence has been explored regarding those fort sites believed built or occupied by the Ninth Legion and newly identified, or potential sites are also considered. Plans of forts have been used and where available, Some GIS mapping has been applied to show the fort superimposed in the correct location over the modern day settlement or topography.

Several theories relating to the eventual demise of the Legion are analysed and discussed in the light of the latest archaeological evidence. These too have then been re-examined and a clear line drawn between what is known from the evidence and what can only be inferred or hypothesised. Suggestions have been made on the most likely explanation for the Ninth's disappearance but still, there is no definitive evidence to prove whether these are correct.

With regard to limitations it is true to say that the data gathering for the project has not been as comprehensive in all respects as was hoped for. The main problem arose in connection with obtaining digital images of the various artefacts from the museums or organisations acting as their custodians. Extensive efforts were made over an eight month period to gather digital images of artefacts but this was particularly challenging as a number of the institutions were in other countries meaning many responses when received, needed some further clarification. In the event, very few of those outside of the United Kingdom actually responded despite repeated requests meaning that the image section of the archive is only about 50% complete.

There are a number of indicators as to where more extensive archaeological work could be beneficial. Perhaps the most valuable would be to conduct full investigations of some of the bases of the Ninth Legion. Malton, in North Yorkshire could prove to contain valuable information. A large number of Roman artefacts have already been found in the area and many more may remain hidden. Some small sections of the outer wall have been excavated but this is a very small percentage of the whole area. The interior is untouched.

Additionally, if excavations were to take place at other sites in Carlisle, Old Carlisle and Scalesceugh (all of which have significant portions accessible from public land or farm land) this might well provide dateable evidence to place the Ninth Legion in Cumbria after AD 108. That would be a very significant step forward in plotting the deployment of the Legion in the final years of its existence. Finally, Siscia in Croatia was a base for the Ninth for a period of 100 years (43 BC to AD 43) and has been barely explored. A significant portion could be accessed comparatively easily and could reveal evidence of significant value to understanding the early history of the Legion.

In terms of learning from carrying through this project, perhaps the most obvious lesson has been that the scope of the project was probably too wide Where to start and where to end are the simplest questions for a study of this length both in terms of time available and the writing period for recording its results; but the temptation to explore further is almost irresistible. Just collating the vast number of different aspects of archaeology of the Ninth requires a huge amount of research and a great deal of time. This was almost certainly too ambitious. Sourcing images was very expensive in terms of time and one learns quickly that if a project requires the cooperation of others, a very long lead in time is needed to achieve your objective.

Persistence did pay off in some area. A considerable cohort of individuals were extremely helpful and many provided tangible pointers to other sources. With regard the images, true - it may have been more sensible to accept defeat at an earlier stage thus leaving more time for writing.

This project may largely succeed in its aim of bringing together opinion and archaeological evidence relating to the Ninth Legion and might prove to be of some value to anyone conducting a future study, in that a significant portion of the 'ground work' will already have been completed. This monograph also provides pointers as to where the relevant evidence can be located and presents information about forts occupied by the Ninth in an accessible visual format. In addition, the discussion of recent evidence and some reinterpretation of the various theories, has hopefully made a useful contribution to the archaeological and historical debate on the fate of the Ninth.

Perhaps of greater importance is the fact this study has helped highlight the consequences for archaeology when opinion or interpretation comes to be valued more highly that the actual evidence on which that opinion or interpretation was originally based. Haalebos' misinterpretation of the stratigraphy at Nijmegen spawned a number of theories about the deployment of the Ninth Legion which were for some time firmly held though based on limited evidence and on dating. These have now been shown to be wrong. This may well have diverted attention from other areas of enquiry which might have proved more valuable. Of some similarity, Richmond's influential assertion (1955) that 'The legion was cashiered, there is no doubt', undermined the work of other eminent archaeologists despite once again there being no firm evidence to prove his views were correct. It may well be that Archaeology's best chance of solving the riddle of what happened to the Ninth Legion is to continue to search for reliable evidence; and to trust in that alone?

For almost two thousand years then, the secrets of Rome's missing Ninth Legion have been shrouded by the mists of time. The VIIII Legio Hispana's ultimate fate has been argued over by generations of historians. The loss of the Ninth Legion was by any measure a truly catastrophic event, so dramatic it saw the devastating news suppressed by Hadrian to safeguard his reign in a classic conspiracy and cover up. The loss of the Ninth was the first in a chain reaction of disasters which forced Rome to halt its expansion and create the only two massive frontier walls ever built in the Roman Empire. Written sources and a raft of evidence from archaeology show how and where the Ninth met its end in the tribal badlands of northern Britain.

In a stunning reveal, archaeologists show how Hadrian first built this huge innovative timber structure to protect the Roman territory to the south before consolidating the construction with stone. Even before this final stone wall was completed, Hadrian despatched his most experienced generals, including the infamous Julius Severus, a ruthless soldier who perfected devastating new tactics against all insurgents; but beyond the frontier, tribes formed powerful new alliances and harried the Roman military in a guerrilla war of attrition.

Over fifteen wars were fought. Three Roman generals and an estimated twenty thousand troops (and more) died fighting hostile tribes, while vast resources were ploughed into trying to maintain Rome's vulnerable frontier system. The might of Rome was waning - the annihilation of the Ninth Legion was most likely the writing on the wall. This was indeed, the beginning of the end!

At the end however, the Ninth legion went on to live in mysterious infamy but with one further mystery left unexplained. Around AD 165 the Emperor Marcus Aurelius commissioned a pair of columns listing every Roman legion and its location throughout the empire. The Ninth 'Hispana' and Twenty Second 'Deiotariana' were nowhere to be seen. This anomaly provides us with a window of time. Between the years AD 108 and AD 165, the Ninth appears to all intent and purpose, to have marched off the imperial records. In normal circumstances, Rome's treatment for disgraced or defeated units would see those legions involved, subject to the 'damnatio memoriae' - the act of removing all record from any of the monuments its name had ever been inscribed. However, as far as we know, there is no evidence of this happening to those monuments identified as relating to the Ninth so again we ask –

'What exactly did happen to the Ninth Legion Hispana?'

Bibliography:

Alföldy, G. & Preussische Akademie der Wissenschaften, A. der W. der D., Berlin-Brandenburgische Akademie der Wissenschaften, 1995. *Corpus inscriptionum Latinarum*, Berlin [u.a.]: de Gruyter.

Askew, G., 1949. A Roman graffito from the City of London. *The Antiquaries Journal*, 29(1-2), pp.84–84.

BBC, 1977. *The Eagle of the Ninth*,

Bennett, S.L., 2010. *Last of the Ninth* 1st ed., Gatineau, Québec: Deux Voiliers Publishing.

Betts, I.M., 1985. *A scientific investigation of the brick and tile industry of York in the mid-eighteenth century*. Ph.D. University of Bradford. Available at: http://hdl.handle.net/10454/2690 [Accessed March 12, 2014].

Bidwell, P. & Hodgson, N., 2009. *The Roman Army in Northern England*, Arbeia Society.

Birley, A.R., 1981. *The fasti of Roman Britain*, Oxford; New York: Clarendon Press ; Oxford University Press.

Birley, A.R., 2005. *The Roman Government of Britain*, OUP Oxford.

Birley, E.B., 1948. *Britain after Agricola, and the end of the Ninth Legion*, [Durham University].

Birley, E.B., 1971. *The Fate of the Ninth Legion* First Edition edition. R. M. Butler, ed., Leicester: Leicester University.

Birley, R., Blake, J. & Birley, A., 1998. *The 1997 excavations at Vindolanda: The Praetorium site interim report*, Greenhead: Roman Army Museum Publications.

Bishop, M.C., 2013a. *Handbook to Roman Legionary Fortresses* 1st ed., Barnsley: Pen & Sword Military.

Bishop, M.C., 2013b. Roman Legionary Fortresses. Available at: http://legionaryfortresses.info/index.htm [Accessed May 8, 2014].

Bogaers, J.E. & Haalebos, J.K., 1979. *Die Nijmegener Legionslager Seit 70 Nach Christus*, Rheinland-Verlag GMBH.

Browning, I., 1989. *Petra* New edition., Chatto & Windus.

Burn, A.R., 1969. *The Romans in Britain: an anthology of inscriptions;*, Oxford: Blackwell.

Caesar, J., 2006. *Galic Wars* 1st ed., Folio Society.

Caesar, J., 2008. *The Civil War* Reissue edition., Oxford ; New York: Oxford Paperbacks.

Campbell, D., 2013. The Fate of the Ninth; The curious disappearance of Legio VIIII Hispana. *Ancient Warfare*, 4(5), p.6.

Cassius Dio, 1987. *The Roman History* Reprint edition., Harmondsworth, Middlesex, England ; New York, N.Y., U.S.A: Penguin Classics.

Churchill, W.S., 1956. *A History of the English-Speaking Peoples*, New York: Skyhorse Publishing.

Cockrell, A., 1979. *The Legions of the Mist: A Novel of Roman Britain* 1st edition., New York: Atheneum.

Collingwood R.G., R.G. & Wright R.P., R.P., 1995. *The Roman Inscriptions of Britain: Instrumentum Domesticum v.2: Volumes 1-8 plus index.*, Sutton Publishing.

Collingwood, R.G. & Wright, R.P., 1983. *The Roman Inscriptions Of Britain: Inscriptions on Stone v1*, Alan Sutton Publishing Ltd.

Dando-Collins, S., 2010. *Legions of Rome: The definitive history of every Roman legion* First Edition., Quercus.

Dessau, H., 2009. *Inscriptiones Latinae Selectae*, BiblioLife.

Dobson, B., 1978. *Die Primipilares. Entwicklung und Bedeutung, Laufbahnen und Persönlichkeiten eines römischen Offiziersranges*, Bonn: Köln : Rheinland-Verlag,.

Driessen, M.D., 2009. The early Flavian timber castra and the Flavian-Trajanic stone legionary fortress at Nijmegen (The Netherlands). In *Limes XX: Estudios sobre la frontera romana (Roman frontier studies)*. Leon. Spain: Editorial CSIC - CSIC Press.

Faulkner, N., 2001. *The Decline and Fall of Roman Britain* New Ed edition., Stroud: The History Press.

Forum Ancient Coins, 2013. Forum Ancient Coins. *Forum Ancient Coins*. Available at: http://www.forumancientcoins.com/ [Access May 14, 2014].

Frere, S.S. et al., 1974. The Roman Fortress at Longthorpe. *Britannia*, 5, p.1.

Fronto, M.C., 2012. *The correspondence of Marcus Cornelius Fronto with Marcus Aurelius Antoninus, Lucius Verus, Antoninus Pius, and various friends;*, Ulan Press.

Goldsworthy, A., 2011. *The Complete Roman Army* Reprint edition., London: Thames and Hudson Ltd.

Greenhalgh, P., 1980. *Pompey: The Roman Alexander v. 1*, London: Littlehampton Book Services Ltd.

Haalebos, J.K., 2000. *Roman Troops in Nijmegen*, Nijmegen: Kathholieke Universiteit Nijmegen.

Hassall, M.W.C., Tomlin, R.S.O. & Wright, R.P., 2009. *The Roman Inscriptions of Britain: Inscriptions on Stone (1955-2006) v. 3*, Oxbow Books.

Higham, N. & Jones, B., 1991. *The Carvetii* Revised edition., Gloucester: Sutton Publishing Ltd.

Highways Agency, 1994. Area 14 Archaeological Reports - Highways Agency. Available at: http://www.highways.gov.uk/our-road-network/archaeology/library-of-archaeological-reports/area-14-archaeological-reports/ [Accessed May 13, 2014].

Horsley, J., 1732. *Britannia Romana: or the Roman antiquities of Britain: in three books*, Gale ECCO, Print Editions.

Jarrett, M.G., 1976. An Unnecessary War. *Britannia*, 7, p.145.

Jones, M.J., 2002. *Roman Lincoln: Conquest, Colony and Capital: Fortress, Colony and Capital*, The History Press LTD.

Kearsley, S., 1997. *The Shadowy Horses*, London: ALLISON & BUSBY.

Keppie, L.J.F., 1998. *The making of the Roman army: from republic to empire*, London: Routledge.

Livy, T.L.P., 2012. *History of Rome*, Acheron Press.

MacDonald, K., 2011. *The Eagle*, Universal Pictures UK.

Marshall, N., 2010. *Centurion*, 20th Century Fox Home Entertainment.

Mattingly, D., 2007. *An Imperial Possession: Britain in the Roman Empire, 54 BC - AD 409*, London; New York: Penguin.

Moffatt, B.M., 2013. The Ninth Legion. Available at: http://fallingangelslosthighways.blogspot.co.uk/2013/02/the-ninth-legion_21.html [Accessed May 12, 2014].

Mommsen, T., 1885. *Romische Geschichte*, Nabu Press.

Mor, M., 1986. Two Legions: The Same Fate? (The Disappearance of the Legions IX Hispana and XXII Deiotariana). *Zeitschrift für Papyrologie und Epigraphik*, 62, pp.267–278.

Olly, M. & Aspin, J., 2011. *The Disappearing Ninth Legion: A Popular History*, O Books.

Ottaway, P., 1996. *Archaeology of York V.3/3: Excavations and observations on the defences and adjacent sites, 1971-90 2 parts*, Council for British Archaeology.

Ottaway, P., 2004. *Roman York*, The History Press Ltd.

Ottaway, P., 2013. *Roman Yorkshire: People, Culture & Landscape*, United Kingdom: Blackthorn Press.

Parker, H.M.D., 1994. *Roman Legions* New edition., New York: Barnes & Noble Inc.

Ramm, H., 1978. *The Parisi*, London: Sutton Publishing Ltd.

Richmond, I., 1955. *Roman Britain* 1st Edition edition., London : Collins.

Ritterling, E., 1925. *Legio*, Nabu Press.

Royal Commission on Historical Monuments, 1995. *Roman Camps in England: The Field Archaeology*, London: Stationery Office Books.

Russell, M., 2010. *Bloodline: The Celtic Kings of Roman Britain*, Amberley Publishing.

Russell, M., 2011. What happened to Britain's Lost Roman Legion? *BBC History Magazine*, pp.40–45.

Salway, P., 1993. *The Oxford illustrated history of Roman Britain*, Oxford; New York: Oxford University Press.

Sansom, D.M., 2010. Ninth Legion. Available at: http://www.erminestreetguard.co.uk/Ninth%20Legion.htm [Accessed September 12, 2013].

Sicker, M., 2000. *The Pre-Islamic Middle East*, Praeger.

Sijpesteijn, P.J., 1996. Die Legio Nona Hispana In Nijmegen. *aus: Zeitschrift für Papyrologie und Epigraphik*, (111), pp.281–282.

Stanier, T., 1965. The Brigantes and the Ninth Legion. *Phoenix*, 19(4), p.305.

Stevens, C.E., 1966. *the building of hadrian's wall*, Society of Antiquaries for Newcastle upon Tyne.

Suetonius, 2007. *The Twelve Caesars* Rev. Ed. / edition., London: Penguin Classics.

Sutcliff, R. et al., 1956. *A Home Service radio dramatisation of The Eagle of the Ninth*, S.I.: BBC Audiobooks Ltd.

Sutcliff, R., 1954. *The Eagle of The Ninth* 1st Edition., OUP Oxford.

Sutcliff, R. & BBC Radio 4, F., 1996. *The Eagle of the Ninth*, North Kingstown, R.I.: BBC Audiobooks Ltd.

Tacitus & Levene, D.S., 2008. *The Histories*, Oxford ; New York: Oxford Paperbacks.

Tacitus, P.G.C., 1967. *Agricola* 2nd edition., Oxford: Oxford University Press.

Tacitus, P.G.C., 2003. *The Annals of Imperial Rome* New Impression edition., Harmondsworth Eng.: Penguin Classics.

Teale, O., 2008. *The Last Legion*, Momentum Pictures.

Watson, G.R., 1969. *The Roman Soldier* First Edition edition., London: Thames & Hudson Ltd.

Weber, W., 1936. *The Cambridge Ancient History 14 Volume Set in 19 Hardback Parts: The Cambridge Ancient History Volume 11: The High Empire, AD 70-192* 1st ed., Cambridge England ; New York, NY, USA: Cambridge University Press.

Webster, G., 1985. *The Roman Imperial Army of the first and second centuries A.D.*, London: Black.

Wenham, L.P., 1974. *Derventio (Malton): Roman Fort and Civilian Settlement*, ABRAMS.

Wilkins, A., 2003. *Roman Artillery*, Princes Risborough: Shire Publications Ltd.

Wright, R.P., 1948. Roman Britain in 1947: I. Sites Explored: II. Inscriptions. *The Journal of Roman Studies*, 38, pp.81–104.

Wright, R.P., 1978. Tile-Stamps of the Ninth Legion Found in Britain. *Britannia*, 9, p.379.

Young, B., 2012. *The Eagle has fallen*,